The Legends of
CHELSEA

The Legends of
CHELSEA

SCOTT CHESHIRE

breedon **books**
PUBLISHING

First published in Great Britain in 2003 by
The Breedon Books Publishing Company Limited
Breedon House, 3 The Parker Centre,
Derby, DE21 4SZ.

ISBN 1 85983 358 6

Printed and bound by Butler & Tanner,
Frome, Somerset, England.

Cover printing by Lawrence-Allen Colour Printers,
Weston-super-Mare, Somerset, England.

Contents

Introduction

ASK two Chelsea fans each to compile a list of their favourite 100 players and although many stars would feature on both lists, they'd also come up with different names.

Since 1905 more than 650 players have appeared in senior competitive matches for the Stamford Bridge club

This book lists the personal choice of long-time Chelsea supporter and acclaimed club historian, Scott Cheshire, whose beautifully crafted essays will bring back memories of former players and former glories.

Gianfranco Zola has recently been voted the greatest player in the club's history, and of course Zola is included here. So are 22st goalkeeper Willie Foulke and 'Gatling Gun George' Hilsdon. Also included are Jack Harrow, the first man to clock up 300 appearances for Chelsea, despite losing four seasons to World War One; Jack Cock, who won the Military Medal in that war and then came to Chelsea to score 53 goals in only 110 games for them; record signing – for £6,500 – Andy Wilson, the Scottish international; Vic Woodley, who kept goal for England in 19 consecutive internationals before World War Two halted his record-breaking run; the two Tommys – Walker and Lawton – Scottish and English internationals respectively, both of whom ended their glorious careers at Stamford Bridge.

Ted Drake is also here, the only manager to guide Chelsea to the League championship, in 1955; influential captain John Harris, who spent 14 seasons with Chelsea; centre-forward Roy Bentley captained that 1955 team and is one of the outstanding players in Chelsea's history; Jimmy Greaves and his astonishing goalscoring record – 132 goals in less than 170 games; Bobby Tambling, another record scorer for Chelsea – 202 in 370 games, all before his 29th birthday.

Peter Bonetti, the almost universal choice for Chelsea's best-ever goalkeeper; defender Ron Harris, the Chelsea Chopper and another member of that magical team of the late 1960s and early 70s; Peter Osgood, another great scorer, was the wayward genius of that side; John Hollins was a non-stop dynamo from the moment he got into the side, a month after his 17th birthday.

Midfielder Ray Wilkins was another star from of a clutch of Chelsea youngsters; yet another famous Chelsea goalscorer, Kerry Dixon, stepped up from the Third Division to grace the top flight and play for England.

There are also to players who also served, not great stars but vital contributors to Chelsea's story none the less. Steve Clarke, 400 senior appearances in 11 years at the Bridge, falls into that category. A legend to all Chelsea fans who remember him.

Legends of Chelsea will inform and entertain, settle some arguments and start new ones. Most of all it will evoke memories of great players and great moments in this great club's story.

Ken Armstrong – never a more loyal servant

IN the winter of 1943-44 a young soldier by the name of Lou Ashcroft was posted to the Home Counties for a few months and threw in his lot with Chelsea, making a handful of guest appearances before his unit moved on.

Previously he had been stationed in the Isle of Man and had played Army football in the same team as an 18-year-old former bank clerk by the name of Ken Armstrong, who had played for his local club, Bradford Rovers, before being called up.

It was while playing, fleetingly, for Chelsea that Ashcroft mentioned Ken's name to Chelsea's assistant manager of those days, Joe Shaw.

Summoned to London for a trial, Armstrong made his debut for the Reserves in September 1945, appearing in a 5-0 defeat at the hands of West Ham United's second team. However he stayed on, still in the Army for a few weeks prior to being posted to Germany.

Certainly he had made a firm impression and on demobilisation in December 1946 he signed professional forms for Chelsea.

Armstrong played reserve team football for the remainder of that season before being selected for the first team's opening fixture in August 1947 at Blackpool.

For 10 seasons he remained an automatic choice in the senior side, playing the majority of his games at right-half, where his sound positional sense and well-timed tackles broke up many an enemy raid, before using the ball to set his forwards on the attack.

He was a most polished and stylish performer and it is even today a matter for surprise that he won only one full international cap for England, when he starred in his country's 7-2 victory against Scotland at Wembley in 1955, even though he was then only called upon after the original choice for his position withdrew through injury.

Week in, week out Ken's contribution was taken for granted. Always ready to answer his manager's call and instructions, whenever an emergency arose.

In April 1951 a crisis loomed with Chelsea needing to win their last four matches to have even a hope of avoiding relegation. Since 14 matches had passed since their last victory, their prospects were far from rosy.

In desperation, manager Billy Birrell moved Armstrong, this time into the inside-left position. Chelsea promptly won the first of those fixtures, at home to Liverpool, 1-0, and followed this up with three victories in each of the remaining games in which Armstrong, clearly not out of his depth, scored three of the eight goals.

For a short time the following season he continued in the forward line before returning to occupy the number-four shirt for the rest of his career

And how appropriate it was that he was still occupying his post in the famous Football League championship season of 1954-55, when he missed only three games. Others may have attracted bigger headlines; none could have exceeded his dependability.

In October 1947 the sudden departure of England centre-forward Tommy Lawton had left Chelsea without an obvious replacement. But, nothing daunted, Armstrong took over the number-nine shirt until a permanent replacement was signed and ended the season as joint leading goalscorer

Retiring unobtrusively in April 1957 with a then club record of 402 first-team appearances, he emigrated with his family to New Zealand, briefly continuing to play before becoming a national coach.

Never had Chelsea had better value for money from a £10 signing-on fee. And they never had a more loyal servant than Ken Armstrong, whose ashes were strewn on the Stamford Bridge pitch after his death in June 1984.

Chelsea Career

402 appearances   30 goals

Benjamin Howard Baker – an extraordinary sportsman

IT is no exaggeration to claim that Benjamin Howard Baker was the most remarkable character to represent Chelsea down the years, overshadowing even Willie Foulke. No one could approach his versatility and all-round ability, not only on the football field but also in a wide variety of other sporting activities.

He was one of the old Corinthians and kept goal for them on 176 occasions (itself a club record) including the legendary FA Cup-tie against Blackburn Rovers in which, not least as a result of his fine display, the First Division professionals were defeated 1-0 at Crystal Palace in 1924.

Twice he appeared for England in full professional internationals as well as being his county's regular amateur 'keeper. More unusually, he was selected for the Football League against the Irish League in 1925.

Fitted into these commitments were almost 100 first-team appearances for Chelsea spread over five seasons: a total severely limited by other sporting demands.

How he would have adapted to the present day game is a fascinating speculation.

On the slightest excuse, and sometimes without reason, he would leave his goal and dash beyond his penalty area to repulse an attack.

For the Corinthians he would charge upfield for corner kicks if the situation was urgent and for a time was their regular penalty-kicker.

Just twice he was given that responsibility for Chelsea. Having scored the only goal of the game against Bradford City from the spot in November 1921, he was less successful on the next occasion and was engaged in a hectic dash back to protect his goal as opponents sped away to take advantage of his absence.

Needless to say the crowd adored such antics and individuality. Indeed, he was a magnetic attraction wherever he played.

From 1921 to 1926 he played in roughly half Chelsea's first-team games; in other words, whenever he made himself available.

His athleticism made him a wonderful stopper of shots, but equally, and maybe surprisingly in view of his style, he was seldom prone to elementary errors.

Crowds everywhere adored him and were fascinated by his antics. A particularly long kicker of the ball, it was by no means unusual for such clearances to reach the opposing goal-line at the other end of the park.

This extraordinary man also represented Great Britain in the Olympic Games of 1912 and 1920 – he was also British high jump champion, once setting a national record – as well as excelling in tennis, water-polo and high diving.

Latterly living in the West Country, his wide range of trophies accumulated in his versatile career was a magnet for sportsmen and made fascinating viewing.

Visitors were always welcome and he liked nothing better than to reminisce about his Stamford Bridge days.

Chelsea Career

93 appearances   1 goal

Tommy Baldwin – an unsung hero

IN discussions about one of Chelsea's most distinguished periods, which embraced winning both the FA Cup and the European Cup-winners' Cup, the name of Tommy Baldwin is sometimes overlooked. Certainly he rarely attracted the headlines in the way that some of his more flamboyant colleagues did; nor did he establish quite the same rapport with the fans.

Yet his contribution was never less than wholehearted and, by his loyalty over nine seasons, unquestioned.

Baldwin was 'on parade' doing his bit in the legendary 1970 FA Cup Final and replay, at Wembley and Old Trafford, and in Athens the following year, a period in which Chelsea's first two major Cup trophies were won.

It was a part-exchange deal, in September 1966, which saw George Graham being transferred to Arsenal while Baldwin moved in the opposite direction to Stamford Bridge.

First he had to convince the fans of his new club, since Graham had been both successful and popular in his stay of just over two years at the Bridge. But all the world likes an 100 per cent trier and this hurdle was soon to be cleared.

Not the least of Baldwin's obvious virtues was his prodigious work-rate, which one or two of the so-called 'big-names' around him did not always share.

He was always available to pick up long passes out from defence and cleverly find the open spaces. Not for nothing was he dubbed 'the Sponge'. He was adept at retaining the ball in a congested area and shielding it from opponents before awaiting the arrival of a colleague stealing into open space.

Inevitably during his early years at the Bridge, he could not compete with Bobby Tambling as a goalscorer. But, nevertheless his strike rate over the ensuing years was on a par with both Peter Osgood and Ian Hutchinson, his fellow strikers in those days.

And some of his goals were saved for important moments. In a brutal FA Cup replay against Burnley, at Turf Moor, on an inhospitable foggy north Lancashire night, he headed a crucial goal to put Chelsea into the lead in extra-time and keep the Blues alive en route to Wembley. Other goals in European football, in Sofia, and against RFC Bruges, were equally notable.

Then, as Chelsea's most famous and most successful team up to that point began to fall apart, Tommy Baldwin stayed with the sinking ship and would undoubtedly have played a more important role in steering the club through those turbulent times. Alas, a most unfortunate injury virtually terminated his Football League career at the age of 30.

But not quite. Tommy Docherty, always one of Baldwin's admirers, enticed him on loan to Old Trafford in January 1975, as Manchester United were coming to terms with life in the Second Division. After only two games, however, it was clear that he was simply not fit enough to compete at that level and a most worthy League career was over apart from brief stops at Millwall (loan), where his name appeared on the League scoresheet for the last time, and Brentford.

It was his seasons at Stamford Bridge that provided the central and most successful part of Tommy Baldwin's career.

Chelsea Career:

228 appearances   92 goals

Joe Bambrick – a brainy footballer

TYPICAL of manager Leslie Knighton's policy of recruiting centre-forwards throughout his six years in charge during the1930s was the signing of the Irish international, Joe Bambrick.

Admittedly Andy Wilson had retired, and Hughie Gallacher had left, but George Mills had already been earmarked as a potential international (he subsequently won three caps and marked his England debut with a hat-trick).

Be that as it may, Joe Bambrick crossed the Irish Sea in time to make his Chelsea debut on Christmas Day 1934, failing to score in a 2-0 victory over Aston Villa.

Despite that barren start for Bambrick, Mills was forgotten and rarely found favour again during the Irishman's stay at Stamford Bridge, other than when injury kept the new man on the sidelines.

Joe (christened James) had built up a formidable reputation as a marksman. In one season alone he had scored 94 goals for his club side, Linfield, in the Irish League.

Then, stepping up into his national team in 1930, he was instrumental in leading the Irish to their biggest win in an international, 7-0 against Wales, the debutant scoring six of the goals.

It was one of the most remarkable international debuts of all time and, not surprisingly, he was afterwards presented with the match ball by the Welsh captain who, despite his obvious disappointment, made a suitable speech to mark the occasion. Another two Bambrick hat-tricks for Ireland were to follow.

Yet, somehow, Joe never really settled into English football, despite a highly respectable goals-to-game ratio (37 from 66 appearances).

He was essentially a brainy footballer. He liked the game played at his preferred pace and it often appeared as if his physique could never match the tempo of those around him.

A student of the game, he studied especially the art of positional play, moving into the open spaces where he had time to control the ball and direct attacks through accurate distribution. Too often, though, he found himself caught up in the hurly-burly going on around him and was unable to express himself.

One critic felt that he would have been more suited in Scottish football. And Bambrick himself realised he was not adapting to his new environment.

"Football is played much more deliberately in Ireland," he once said. "I have certainly discovered that in England, thought and action have to be more rapidly associated."

Rather than continue to struggle to produce the form which he had found so easy to come by in Irish football, and finding himself relegated into the reserve-team football with Mills again taking over the leadership of the Chelsea attack, he was placed on the transfer list. Now past the age of 30 and his international days over, he was transferred to Walsall in March 1938.

Bambrick's name is permanently installed in the record books, but regrets remain with questions unanswered. Above all, what heights, and records might have been achieved had he remained in his own country?

Yet for a while he was one of Chelsea's best centre-forwards down the years. A complete striker, but never selfish. A leader of the attack in every sense of the word. A most popular man both with his playing colleagues and with spectators.

It was a great pity that in England he never quite met his own high standards or satisfied his targets and ambitions regularly enough.

Chelsea Career

66 appearances   37 goals

George Barber – took an opportunity

DURING the 1930s the cheque book was permanently available to bring top stars from England and Scotland to Stamford Bridge as Chelsea tried desperately to buy success and challenge the supremacy being enjoyed at Highbury by Arsenal.

One signing which most definitely did not come into this category, however, was that of George Barber, a tall, slender full-back who had been sacked by Luton Town in the 1930 close-season.

"Yes, I got the sack," George said later. "Very properly because I was far from being good."

With Les Odell and Tommy Law the recognised first-team full-backs, senior opportunities seemed unlikely. But from the word go the newcomer impressed with the Reserves in the old London Combination.

George became popular with the crowds at those games (around 5,000 every match in those days) for his reliability and 100 per cent effort. And having unexpectedly been offered a contract with a club in the top division, he was determined not to let the opportunity pass him by.

Soon that opportunity beckoned. Within four months of signing, he was summoned to travel to Birmingham and join the first-team party to play at Villa Park on Boxing Day 1930; a vacancy at full-back had been created by an injury to Law.

Chelsea were in sight of victory when a defender conceded a penalty for Villa to level the score. But the new boy had impressed and went on to hold his place in the senior side for the next eight seasons.

"I owed such a lot to Tommy Law," he once said. "I kept trying to do things his way and got endless tips from him."

Somewhat clumsy and awkward in his early days, the rough edges in George's play soon disappeared. His positional sense was excellent; he was an expert in the sliding tackle, always fairly executed, which dispossessed many an unsuspecting opponent. And his clearances were well-directed, with an eye to launching an attack.

By the time World War Two had begun, Barber had clocked up almost 300 first-team appearances before, in the autumn of 1941 and at the age of 32, he called it a day.

The moment of truth had arrived when, now of course no longer engaged in daily training, the Chelsea defence was overrun by a rampant Millwall side at The Den, conceding six goals at that old ground.

Nevertheless, George Barber was certainly entitled to walk away proud of his service to Chelsea.

An interesting man, he held the firm opinion that a professional footballer must have other interests and options.

"The average modern player is a more educated fellow than those of years ago," he once said. "Nowadays he has too much common sense to take up a profession which has no guarantee for his future. Clubs should permit their players to do outside work."

Having starting his life in football with Fairbairn House, he had longed to combine the winter game with professional cricket for his native county, Essex. But it was not to be.

However he did become a talented artist, self-taught, and had carefully prepared for his retirement.

Chelsea Career

294 appearances   1 goal

Dave Beasant – "...can't believe he's still going"

FEW players in the modern game have served, and survived, League football longer than Dave Beasant. Joining Wimbledon in August 1979, he was part of the team's legendary rise from Fourth Division stragglers to top-flight status and, of course, their epic FA Cup victory at Wembley against Liverpool in 1988.

Just over seven months later Chelsea paid a then record fee of £725,000 to Newcastle United – Beasant had been on Tyneside for six months – to fill their goalkeeping vacancy caused by the career-ending injury to Eddie Niedzwiecki.

Dave made two international appearances for England at a time when manager Graham Taylor was experimenting, in order to find a permanent successor to Peter Shilton.

At Stamford Bridge he at once became a big favourite with the fans, despite operating behind a somewhat improvised and inexperienced defence which, as Beasant himself confessed, "tended to give away silly goals at the back." This undoubtedly caused England to look elsewhere for their permanent last line of defence.

Beasant will always be remembered for his successful record in saving penalty-kicks, gaining this reputation following his crucial save in that 1988 FA Cup Final.

"There is more to saving them than some people think, but you can get a good idea from the way players run up to the ball where they are going to put it. That is the key stage because you have virtually no time to reach the shot once it has been taken."

His goalkeeping style was flamboyant and he was never afraid to come swiftly off his line, even if on occasions it proved costly, such judgements not always being wise or successful. It was this sometime fallibility which caused him to be replaced temporarily by Kevin Hitchcock in the 1991–92 season, before he left Chelsea altogether in November 1992 when he moved to Southampton for a £300,000 fee.

During latter days of uncertainty Beasant conducted himself with great dignity, even though he never quite succeeded in rebuilding his relationship with the fans.

By then, too, Dmitri Kharine had arrived and the highly competent Kevin Hitchcock was also at hand.

But Dave was not a quitter. At Southampton he made almost a century of first-team appearances spread over five seasons.

Next stop, at the age of 37, was Nottingham Forest where he remained their undisputed first choice in goal for another four campaigns, playing around 150 games, while in the 2002–03 season he was still on the end of a telephone ready to answer any club crisis, even though he was nudging the age of 43.

If he had left Stamford Bridge in not altogether happy circumstances it was not a final farewell.

At the turn of the century he was training with Chelsea and in January 2000 took his final bow on the stage in Fulham Road, playing for Nottingham Forest in a fourth-round FA Cup-tie.

As Dennis Wise put it, "Bez is back then. I can't believe he's still going... he was old when I was 17."

And, although Forest lost the tie 2-0, Dave Beasant received a rapturous welcome from his former fans, cheering his every move. He left the stage smiling.

Chelsea Career

157 appearances

Roy Bentley – Chelsea's most influential player?

THERE can never be a unanimous verdict as to who has been Chelsea's 'greatest-ever'. But the most influential? And whose name has survived through the generations of supporters most vividly?

Certainly Roy Bentley is as often mentioned and unanimously recognised on his still regular visits to Stamford Bridge, as anyone from a bygone era.

And, as captain of Chelsea's only Football League championship side, this is scarcely surprising.

A man of the South-West, born in Bristol, he cut his teeth with both Rovers and City before being transferred to Tyneside where, playing at inside-right, he became a member of one of the most successful and talented forward lines in Newcastle United's history.

Then, in January 1948, Chelsea obtained his services for an £11,000 fee, a transfer deal later to prove one of their most successful ever.

Not always recalled, his early days at Stamford Bridge were far from successful. Somehow he didn't seem to fit into the manager's scheme of things, In fact, Bentley recalled later, "I almost felt like packing up."

And then, at the start of his second season an injury to regular centre-forward, Hugh Billington, saw Roy taking over as leader of the attack.

In his first home game in that position he bagged a couple of goals in a 6-0 massacre of Everton. And by the end of that season, absent on only two occasions, he had totted up 21 goals, plus two in FA Cup-ties.

Initially he was given a roving commission, unsettling defenders who seemed nonplussed and uncertain on how to combat what were then unorthodox methods of attack. A year or two later, having made his name and been recognised by the England selectors, he returned to operate almost entirely in the centre of the attack.

Seemingly possessing a spring in his boots he was a brilliant header of the ball, climbing above taller opponents, hovering, before directing the ball past the goalkeeper.

Speed and acceleration were other assets and preceded many of his goals, scored venomously from either foot.

His England days embraced the years from 1949 to 1955, the most famous of his nine goals being that scored against Scotland in a 1-0 victory and providing the passport to the 1950 World Cup in South America.

But his biggest, and of course best recalled, triumph was at Chelsea, leading the legendary 1955 championship side. Even now he happily recalls that season and its marvellous climax.

Having climbed from mid-table anonymity in October, Chelsea then played 24 games leading up to the winning of the title and they included 14 victories and six draws. They were possibly aided by an early elimination from the FA Cup in February.

The crowds flocked in with an aggregate of 1,017,451 all told. Over 75,000 saw the crucial home game with nearest rivals, Wolves, at Easter.

Indeed they were heady days never to be forgotten by those then supporting the club, with the climax coming with victory clinching the title in the last home game.

"I could have wept" recalled Roy afterwards "I was so happy to hear those Chelsea cheers. That wonderful crowd. They had taken it on the chin for 50 years and always come up smiling."

And Roy Bentley is still a regular, and most welcome, visitor to Stamford Bridge to the present day.

Chelsea Career

367 appearances   150 goals

Frank Blunstone – cool as an old campaigner

SOME players take time to settle into a new environment, to find their bearings and establish a rapport with new colleagues and, not least, with the fans.

Not so Frank Blunstone. He was only 18 when he arrived at Stamford Bridge, having been introduced to professional football in his home town, with Crewe Alexandra.

He was an 'old-fashioned' winger "They stuck me out there so that I could keep out of trouble," was his explanation.

Manager Ted Drake signed Blunstone for Chelsea in February 1953, obviously with an eye to build for the future.

But Frank was not kept on the sidelines for long. Within weeks he played his first senior game, against Tottenham Hotspur at White Hart Lane, immediately impressing Charles Buchan, the legendary former England international and a leading journalist of the day.

Buchan wrote, 'Chelsea's prospects of avoiding relegation have been improved by the discovery of a young promising left winger. Cool as an old campaigner, he showed he has craft in his feet.'

Blunstone marked his debut that day by calmly beating Spurs' England goalkeeper Ted Ditchburn with a neat lob to earn Chelsea a 1-1 draw.

For 12 seasons Frank Blunstone was Chelsea's outside-left and his total of almost 350 first-team appearances would have been considerably greater (as indeed would his total of five international caps for England), had he not twice suffered hairline fractures of a leg which caused him to be out of action for 16 months.

He was never a prolific goalscorer. Rather his role was to create chances for his fellow strikers.

An old-fashioned dribbler, head down, he would weave his way past defenders on the flanks, on either outside or inside, before drawing others out of position from the centre to create goalscoring opportunities with his pin-point crosses.

Such as Roy Bentley, Ron Tindall, Bobby Tambling and Barry Bridges owed him a rich debt.

Despite his legendary status at Stamford Bridge, it is a matter of speculation to wonder how far he might have gone had circumstances been kinder.

His appearances in the 1954–55 Football League championship side were limited by his National Service in the Army (22864291 Private Blunstone)

His England call-ups would have been more frequent had his career not coincided with the era of Stanley Matthews and Tom Finney.

And then, of course, there was the loss of almost two complete seasons through injury, when Frank was in his mid-20s.

Indeed, it was yet another set-back which finally ended his career at the age of 30, after he damaged an Achilles tendon in a summer tour in the May 1964. He never played first-class football again.

It was his friend and close colleague Eric Parsons who spoke for many.

"It was a pleasure to play on the same side as Frank. A most kindly and unassuming lad off the field, but on the field a first-class player with a wonderful sense of ball control. He always gave 100 percent... a player I would have on my side any day."

Chelsea Career

347 appearances   54 goals

Peter Bonetti – enter 'The Cat'

AS the centenary of Chelsea Football Club draws near, the line of players who have guarded their net down the years naturally lengthens. And that line is, indeed, a highly distinguished one.

Top of the list, at any rate if a recent supporters' poll is the definitive authority, is Peter Bonetti. Some elders may advance the claims of others, but few could seriously argue the choice, apart from possibly Vic Woodley.

Bonetti's Chelsea career spanned 20 seasons during which only once was his position temporarily usurped.

Dependability and brilliance are not always bedfellows so far as goalkeepers are concerned but in Bonetti's case this was true.

Rare, indeed, were his errors. Invariably during almost every game his brilliance surfaced.

It was a happy and auspicious day when Peter's mother wrote to the Chelsea secretary to request a trial for her son. A letter which not only settled her boy's' career but also helped to determine the most successful, and most colourful, era in the club's history up to that time.

The first occasion when he pulled on his green jersey was in a South-East Counties League game in February 1958; a new chapter in Chelsea's history had begun.

Ted Drake was the club's manager at that time. His championship side was broken, withered by age, and their successors were lesser men, partly untried and certainly unreliable.

Having won his spurs with the Juniors, including an FA Youth Cup winners' medal, and a somewhat brief apprenticeship in the Combination team, Bonetti was parachuted into the League side on 2 April 1960, a fixture at Stamford Bridge against Manchester City.

The previous 18 games had produced three wins as against ten defeats. Relegation was not merely a possibility but a 'bookmaker's favourite'. However, not only did Chelsea chalk up a comfortable 3-1 win, the rookie goalkeeper also performed impeccably and his place in the side was confirmed in the following five games, two of which were won and one drawn, and Chelsea's place in the top division assured.

And so Peter Bonetti's undisputed 15-year reign as Chelsea's goalkeeper began.

Over this period few would argue that week in, week out, Bonetti ('The Cat') was the best, and most dependable club goalkeeper in England.

His mere seven full international caps for England do him scant justice. At first Ron Springett was in charge of his country's last line of defence after which Gordon Banks was the selector's first choice. Sadly, so far as international football goes Bonetti is somewhat unfairly linked with England's World Cup elimination in Mexico in 1970.

Many are the memories of his breathtaking skills with Chelsea: his gracefulness and wonderfully secure catching in dealing with high balls, plucking them from the sky with assured certainty; his speed off his goal-line to narrow an angle. He was supremely fit, a natural athlete.

One of his greatest nights came in the FA Cup Final replay against Leeds United at Old Trafford in April 1970.

Comparatively early in that game he was felled in a collision with an opponent. For seemingly endless minutes he received treatment on the pitch surrounded by a circle of worried teammates.

Resuming at length he was beaten almost immediately as Leeds took the lead but thereafter, almost hobbling on his one sound leg, made two especially fine saves to first keep Chelsea in the game and later preserve their 2-1 lead shortly before the final whistle.

It is no coincidence that Peter Bonetti was Chelsea's goalkeeper in one of the most successful period in their history

Chelsea Career
729 appearances

John Bumstead – team man in a team game

BORN in Rotherhithe, John Bumstead was a natural sportsman. "I was always keen on every sport at school, although I wasn't so keen on running. Pole-vaulting was my big thrill... but the trouble was that it took place on a Saturday morning and clashed with football, so I gave it up."

Athletics' loss was Chelsea Football Club's gain. Bumstead joined Chelsea as a 13-year-old schoolboy in 1971, became an apprentice in July 1975 and turned professional 18 months later.

Immediately taken to the hearts of Stamford Bridge supporters, he was an energetic, wholehearted non-stop runner in midfield, strong in the tackle and constructive in his distribution, his long passes frequently opening opposing defences.

He was an ideal 'team man' in what he once described as 'team game'.

"I don't mind what role I am asked to play. If you are asked to mark somebody and do it well then you derive as much enjoyment out of that as you do pushing forward in a creative role.

"We all have our bits to play. But I do love scoring goals."

All of which epitomised John's outlook on football and his tremendous value to Chelsea.

During his long and honourable reign at Stamford Bridge, he played under no fewer than four managers, versatile enough to respond to fitting into a variety of tactical formations, until injury forced him to call it a day in February 1991.

Probably his most fruitful, and most satisfying, season was that of 1986–87. More than once earlier in his career he had remarked on the fact that his somewhat meagre tally of goals was a disappointment to him (even though he had just found the net no fewer than six times in nine games).

Soon after, his appetite would doubtless have been satisfied by a tally of eight goals in just over three months.

During his long Stamford Bridge career he experienced the usual ups and downs of his profession. His first taste of League football came against Leeds United in November 1978 at Elland Road, followed by the pronouncement that 'John had made a most encouraging debut in midfield' (Chelsea lost 2-1 with all the goals coming in the opening five minutes).

Relegation ensued in the following May after a disastrous spell of 13 defeats in 18 games (one victory), with Bumstead mostly viewing the catalogue of disasters from the substitutes' bench.

By the time promotion was achieved, exactly 12 months after Chelsea almost fell through the trap door into the Third Division, he had become an automatic selection in one of the midfield roles. But, unluckily for him, no major honours came his way and he could only look back on a series of Chelsea's near-misses before he left the Bridge.

Three defeats in the semi-finals of major Cup competitions was an unlucky and frustrating record on which to reflect. But he walked away, proudly, at the end of the 1990–91 season, a man never to be forgotten at Stamford Bridge.

Even then, aged 33, he was not yet quite ready to foresake the game he loved and had served so well.

He signed on for Charlton Athletic and gave further excellent service in their first team for two more seasons after which even John Bumstead was obliged to call time.

Chelsea Career

379-30 appearances   44 goals

Bobby Campbell – like an arrow from a bow

BOBBY Campbell, born in Glasgow, was a teenager when World War Two began in 1939 and he made his mark in Scottish junior football before signing professional forms for Falkirk in 1941.

Aged 24 when normal football resumed in 1946, like all players of his generation he had already lost some of his best playing years to the war.

At that time Chelsea were desperately trying to rebuild their professional staff, virtually all of whom had retired during the hostilities.

With a Scot, Billy Birrell, as Chelsea's manager, naturally use was made of his connections north of the border to scour the market for emerging talent.

Thus Bobby Campbell came to Stamford Bridge in the autumn of the second post-war season, to take over the right-wing berth previously occupied by Dick Spence for almost 13 seasons.

It was immediately clear that Birrell, and his contacts, had done a sound job. In front of a crowd of almost 68,000 spectators, Campbell scored twice on his debut, in Chelsea's 4-2 victory over Aston Villa, on each occasion converting shrewd passes from Len Goulden.

For six seasons he was an automatic first-team choice. Most at home on the right wing, he also had spells on the opposite flank and at inside-forward. He possessed both excellent ball control and speed, and acceleration which opened up defences and gave him the time to place his pin-pointed crosses on to the head of centre-forward Roy Bentley.

But his role was seen mainly as a provider. Nevertheless he was credited with what many in a crowd of over 64,000 claimed to be the most spectacular goal in Chelsea's history, in January 1950.

In a fourth-round FA Cup-tie against Newcastle United on a frozen surface at Stamford Bridge, with Campbell wearing rubber-soled boots into which he had changed at half-time, he fastened on to a loose ball well inside his own half and, within seconds, had put the ball into the net past Newcastle's goalkeeper Jack Fairbrother.

Almost the entire Newcastle team had moved up into the Chelsea penalty area, leaving Bobby a clear 70-yard chase towards goal. Seldom had a ball left one goalmouth and entered the net at the other end of the ground more quickly.

As one correspondent summed it up, "Like an arrow from a bow Campbell streaked for his objective. The crowd roared in excitement as the Geordie left-back hurried off in fruitless pursuit. To maintain footing and control at such a pace seemed utterly impossible. But as goalkeeper Fairbrother rushed into the scene, Campbell ended the day with a low shot which found the far corner of the net."

From the Chelsea half of the field, 19 players watched as if bewitched.

The exertion, nevertheless, had taken its toll. Campbell had felt his leg 'going' during that race down the wing but, rather than succumb to the pain and discomfort (there were, of course, no substitutes in those days), he hobbled along until the final whistle. However, he was then forced to miss the next four League games.

The Scot spent seven seasons at Stamford Bridge, making over 200 appearances on either wing and, occasionally, appearing at inside-forward.

After retiring as a player, he briefly held a coaching appointment with Reading, then in 1960-61 spent 12 months as manager of Dumbarton before moving to Bristol Rovers where he remained for 18 years, first as chief coach and then manager.

Four times he returned to Stamford Bridge with the West Country club, on one occasion rushing on to the field to attend to an injured player with seemingly no loss of his old pace – and to the cheers of the Chelsea fans.

Chelsea Career

213 appearances   40 goals

Steve Clarke – they also serve

IT was indeed a significant moment in Chelsea's history when their Scottish scout suggested that the club should take a look at a young full-back playing for St Mirren.

Initially, the Scottish club's manager dismissed the approach out of hand. But the man was sacked six months later and his successor, interested in one of Chelsea's goalkeepers, was prepared to do business and so an exchange deal was arranged.

Thus, for a fee of £422,000, Steve Clarke embarked on his Stamford Bridge career, beginning with a substitute appearance against Norwich and then making his first full appearance in an FA Cup-tie at Watford where he played centre-back.

He was never a truly great player, rather a sound professional. Always trustworthy, he could, and often did, fill any position in the defence and ever eyeing the chance to break forward into attack.

But he made his name as an outstanding defender, most usually at right-back.

He read the game well, was deceptively quick and an excellent passer of the ball. Always giving 100 per cent, and invariably the first to arrive at the training ground, and usually one of the last to leave.

He was, of course, an integral part of Chelsea's rise from near anonymity to their place among the top clubs in Europe.

Strangely, since Ken Shellito was forced out of the game through injury, Chelsea have often lacked a top-class natural right-back, apart from Gary Locke and, more fleetingly, Paddy Mulligan. And Steve Clarke had to adapt to what was required of him by different managers.

Manager Bobby Campbell clipped his wings and demanded that concentration on defensive duties were paramount, partially relenting later, before Clarke fell out of favour and lost his place in the first team (which probably cost him a chance of playing for Scotland in the World Cup)

It was under Ian Porterfield's managership that Steve won back this first-team slot, which he never relinquished again other than through injuries or illness, apart from a spell when Gareth Hall caused him to be pushed forward into a midfield role.

He was Chelsea's Player of the Year when the club reached their first FA Cup Final for 24 years in 1994. In fact that was probably the height of his Stamford Bridge career.

Excellent performances continued as he widened his repertoire, sometimes appearing on the left of the back three, or as a centre back in a back four and slotting into a diamond formation.

Latterly he was officially appointed vice-captain to Dennis Wise whose unpredictability on and off the field Clarke handled as competently as he did a series of world-class forward opponents.

Chelsea Career

417-14 appearances   10 goals

Jack Cock – the near perfect athlete

BORN in 1895, Jack Cock was one of that group of promising players whose career was dislocated by the outbreak of World War One.

After cutting his teeth with Old Kingstonians and Brentford (his birthplace), he had just joined Huddersfield Town in April 1914 and was slowly establishing himself in their League line-up when the war began and he was called up in the Army and posted to the South of England, before going overseas and eventually winning the Military Medal.

When League football returned to normal in September 1919, he went back to Huddersfield Town but that club was in financial crisis and Chelsea obtained his services by paying a £2,500 fee.

In any case it was always likely, given the opportunity, that he would return to his London roots.

Immediately he filled the centre-forward space vacated by Vivian Woodward (who had retired) and Bob Whittingham, who was not in the best of health and happy to return to his native Staffordshire and sign for Stoke.

Cock had already won an international cap and his impact on the Chelsea team was immediate, scoring on his debut against Bradford (PA) and finishing the season with the impressive tally of 24 goals from 30 first-team games.He was also an influential contributor to Chelsea reaching the FA Cup semi-final that season.

This first season was the highlight of Cock's Stamford Bridge career and his output of goals fell away markedly during the next two years. Consistency was missing from his game, although he remained an automatic first-team choice.

Certainly enthusiasm was never lacking and Jack Whitley, Chelsea's trainer in those day, described him as 'the perfect athlete', but also 'the worry of my life'. Fearing that Cock's energy would burn himself out, he would order him back to the dressing room after training was over. But as soon as Whitley's back was turned, Cock was out on the field again.

Jack Cock possessed exceptional speed, and was an artistic ball player. Many of his goals were spectacular. He could shoot with either foot and was a fine header of the ball.

Although there were no obvious successors to him on the Stamford Bridge pay-roll at that time, he was allowed to move to Everton in January 1923, leaving behind an indelible impression, but one tinged with sadness that he never quite fulfilled his outstanding start.

After moving from Everton to Plymouth Argyle, he returned to London again and signed for Millwall, first as a player (1927–31) when he won a Division Three South championship medal, and then as manager (1944–48).

Once more his path brought him into contact with Chelsea. In the 1943–44 Football League South Cup Final at Wembley, Millwall were the opposition and Jack Cock their recently appointed manager.

Before his death in April 1966, he continued to live in London, for much of the time in Fulham, and never lost interest in the game which he had illuminated years before.

His striking good looks, combined with a fine tenor voice, saw him appearing on the music hall stage when his playing days were over.

Chelsea Career

110 appearances   53 goals

Charlie Cooke – footballer of the highest class

FROM its earliest days Chelsea FC have always aimed to provide top entertainment by signing the type of player who would fill that particular bill and attract the casual, as well as the committed, spectator to Stamford Bridge.

Into this category came Charlie Cooke who, apart from his attraction as a star personality, was a footballer of the highest class.

Few players down the years established a closer relationship with the fans. And few, if any, could have claimed to be greater entertainers.

Charlie, born in Fife, cut his footballing teeth with Renfrew Juniors before graduating up the well-trodden Scottish ladder into their League football, first to Aberdeen, and then Dundee.

In the spring of 1966, for the third season in succession, Chelsea had promised rather more than they had achieved in domestic football. Challenging for the League championship, they were let down by inconsistency and an especially bleak sequence of poor results in the second half of April.

And, for the second season in succession, they were eliminated in the FA Cup at the semi-final stage.

However, in Europe's Inter-Cities Fairs Cup they had reached the semi-final stage and were paired against FC Barcelona.

Coinciding with that vital fixture was the widening rift between manager Tommy Docherty and one of his key players, Terry Venables.

Hastily signed as a replacement, Charlie Cooke found himself making his debut in that competition. It was too late for him to properly settle into his new environment and influence the result, but, none the less, one of Chelsea's greatest players had moved in.

He had already made his mark at the higher level before coming to the Bridge, not least when for Scotland he had mesmerised the English defence at Hampden Park in front of 135,000 spectators.

His total mastery of the ball and his magic trickery bewildered opponents and delighted the fans. He would torment defenders, sometimes repeating the dose against a helpless victim, with his matchless ball conjuring. Few have equalled his dribbling at high speed.

Occasionally he may have left himself open to the criticism that he was showing off his enormous talent at the expense of team interests, but still the crowds adored him.

There were far more positive occasions. Many will always recall the moment in the FA Cup Final replay against Leeds United at Old Trafford, when Charlie's long looping centre neutralised Jackie Charlton and company to present Peter Osgood with the vital equalising goal which turned the whole game to Chelsea's advantage.

But, sadly, it was not to last as that famous team fell apart and the little Scot was transferred to Crystal Palace, in September 1972.

More happily, he returned 17 months later and, if time had blunted some of the speed and sharpness, his class and pedigree were still there and it was a further blow to supporters when he emigrated to the USA.

Until the present day Chelsea have had few greater entertainers. Or few more intelligent personalities. Or many whose memory survives the passage of time.

Chelsea Career

360-13 appearances   30 goals

Allan Craig – a defender all his days

ALREADY approaching the age of 30, and with a string of honours won north of the border with his only other professional club, Motherwell, Allan Craig was transferred to Chelsea for the considerable fee, in those days, of £4,000.

He had played three times for Scotland, including the game against England at Wembley in 1932, won 3-0 by the home team, as well as winning a Scottish League championship medal with Motherwell in the same year, and a Scottish FA Cup runners-up medal the previous season.

For 12 months he competed for his position with Peter O'Dowd, an England international centre-half, at that time considered Chelsea's finest-ever in that position.

But once O'Dowd fell out with the Stamford Bridge manager – and emigrated to France where he spent almost all the rest of his football career (for much greater financial rewards) – Allan Craig became a virtually permanent fixture in the centre of Chelsea's defence, as well as being appointed captain.

Unlike his two immediate predecessors in the centre-half spot – O'Dowd and Jack Townrow – Craig considered his function purely as defensive, rarely making an upfield excursion and being concerned only with obliterating his attackers, and most especially, the opposing centre-forward.

At that time the Chelsea board were more concerned with attracting 'big name' forwards, aimed to fill the 70;000 capacity of Stamford Bridge. Indeed, in Allan's seven seasons with the club only two notable newcomers in defence, both wing-halves – Irish international Billy Mitchell and England's Sam Weaver – were signed.

This at a time when Chelsea could draw on no fewer than three current international centre-forwards, two wingers and two inside-forwards who had also represented their country.

From January 1933 until the outbreak of World War Two, Craig, both captained the team and was the bulwark of the defence.

A most stylish player and, although an inch short of 6ft, he was dominant in the air as well as being a strong tackler.

But was he not one to attract attention. Even his arrival at Stamford Bridge passed without comment in the *Official Programme*.

Only twice was he forced out of the team, missing a large part of the 1937–38 campaign when he was replaced for a time by his loyal, long-serving deputy Bob Griffiths, and again the following season when Bob Salmond was signed from Portsmouth with a view to the future which never arrived due to the outbreak of World War Two.

Yet Allan Craig finished the 1938–39 season back at his post, past the age of 35, and knowing that his contract would not be renewed.

And in this period he appeared in the game for which he is most remembered, if perhaps not happily so. Chelsea, having disposed of Arsenal, Fulham and Sheffield Wednesday (after a second replay) in the FA Cup, were rewarded with a sixth-round tie at home to Grimsby Town, with extravagant talk from the fans of a 'first-ever Wembley' being banded about.

It was Chelsea's 100th FA Cup appearance. The weather was wet and windy, and underfoot playing conditions treacherous. The crowd of 45,000 was lower than for the three previous home ties. And it was soon clear that one goal would almost certainly decide the contest.

Chelsea's defence, marshalled as ever by Craig, was well in control until a cut eye necessitated the centre-half's withdrawal for medical attention. He was off the field for only a matter of a few moments but it was long enough for the appropriately name Fred Crack to settle the tie with the only goal of the game for the visitors.

Chelsea were left to resume their ultimately successful battle against relegation, while Grimsby lost their semi-final tie, 5-0 against Wolverhampton Wanderers at Old Trafford.

Meanwhile, Allan Craig, playing in the last four League games of the season, slipped into honourable retirement.

Chelsea Career
211 appearances

Jackie Crawford – from shipyard to international player

BORN on Tyneside, Jackie Crawford was raised in the shipyard environment of the North-East at the turn of the century.

Like many other Geordies, he began his football with a local team, Palmer's Works (Jarrow), on rough, bare pitches which, if nothing else, was not a bad way to learn the art of ball control. And so well did he progress that he was spotted by a scout for his local league club, Jarrow Town.

Within days he was making his first appearance for that club, in a friendly against Hull City, and was an instant success, so much so that not only did the Yorkshire club immediately sign him on professional forms, they also included him in their Second Division game against Huddersfield Town a few days later, in March 1919.

Having taken the step-up to semi-professional status so easily, Crawford made an equally instant impression with Hull, even though he was playing on the unfamiliar left wing.

From that moment he was an automatic choice for the Tigers, missing only a handful of games, through injury. So conscious of Jackie's Crawford's potential were the home supporters that one was heard to shout out, "Don't score Jackie, or you'll be sold."

Alas for Hull City, too late. Crawford had already been spotted by a Chelsea scout and for the then considerable fee of £3,000, after playing more than 100 games for the Humberside club, he signed for the Londoners in May 1923.

In his stay of more than 10 years at Stamford Bridge he had mixed experiences. At the end of his first season, during which he also figured at inside-forward, Chelsea were relegated to Division Two. But this in no way deterred Jackie. For the next six seasons he was a fixture on his favourite right wing, seldom missing a game through injury.

Loyalty and persistence then gained its reward when he was a regular member of the 1929–30 promotion side.

He was capped once and at Chelsea was the only England player in an all-international forward line.

Already he had surmounted many hurdles, so he settled quickly back in the top flight and in spite of Chelsea constantly producing the cheque book to strengthen the team in their search for honours, Crawford's position was never under threat until, after a prolonged enforced absence through injury, at the age of 37 he was overtaken by Father Time.

Now a converted Londoner, he then signed for Queen's Park Rangers where he stayed for three seasons before retiring at the age of 40.

Popular on the field, he had an infectious sense of humour involving constant practical jokes 'both for and against'.

Once on a railway journey to an away fixture, Crawford, who stood only 5ft 2in, was issued a half-price boy's ticket, which on both outward and return journeys the collector happily clipped, and the joke at Crawford's expense fell flat. On this, and on most other occasions, he proved himself a winner.

Chelsea Career

308 appearances   27 goals

Jimmy Croal – football was his art form

CHELSEA FC directors have seldom been lacking in ambition, and, more than most down the years have been ready to flourish the cheque book.

The summer of 1914 provided a case in point. A clutch of promising signings had been made, some of whom were destined never to make their mark, with the outbreak of World War One bringing more serious matters than professional football.

Among the new entry in August of that year was the Scottish left-wing pair of Jimmy Croal and Bobby McNeil. Together, despite losing four seasons during hostilities, they went on to clock up some 400 first-team games for Chelsea.

As with others from north of the border, they took time to acclimatise to the game in England, but nevertheless were a potent force in steering their new club to their first-ever FA Cup Final.

Jimmy Croal, with three Scottish international caps to his credit, was a true craftsman at inside-left. But, he never enjoyed the more physical up-and-at-'em type of game. For him football was an art form; an activity in which he could display the more leisurely skilful crafts of his profession, which, of course, was a well-known feature in Scottish football.

In two respects he left himself open for his critics. When possession was lost it was just not in his repertoire to fight back to retrieve the situation.

Secondly, for an inside-forward in those days his output of goals scored was perhaps somewhat below normal expectation.

But what he did achieve regularly, and with a mathematical precision, was to lay on scoring opportunities for others. Even then his aim to ensure perfection in achieving such openings brought accusations of slowing down the attack.

Both he and McNeil in partnership, however, certainly delighted their admirers even if at times they did seem to lose sight of the object of the exercise.

On and off the field Jimmy Croal was a quiet man; in action he worked tirelessly rather than entertaining the fans.

En route to the FA Cup Final, having missed the first round and replay through injury, he was present in the other six matches, in fact scoring a vital goal in the semi-final against Everton at Villa Park.

Sadly he was never able to impose his authority in the Final, when the whole team simply did not respond to the occasion: 'As helpless as a reed shaken in the wind; they would not have scored had they played for a week,' one writer summed up.

Croal, despite being 34 when normal football resumed in 1919, occupied the inside-left position for a further three seasons and was at his usual post in the 1921 FA Cup quarter-final against Cardiff City at Ninian Park. Once more the defence out-performed the attack which failed to score

When he left Stamford Bridge in March 1922 he moved down the road to Fulham.

He never returned home to reside in Scotland, but retired to live in a Somerset village, no doubt well-suited to the pace of rural life,. He died there in 1939, sadly by his own hand.

Chelsea Career

130 appearances   26 goals

Ed De Goey – the ideal temperament

AT 6ft 6in, Ed Goey is the tallest man ever to play for Chelsea. Whilst at his previous club, Feyenoord, he came to the attention of manager Ruud Gullit, who lost little time in signing the Dutchman for Chelsea in June 1997 for a £2.25 million fee, the highest amount ever paid for a goalkeeper up to that time.

He had already won 29 international caps for Holland, had plenty of experience of European club football and was ready to step into the shoes of Frode Grodas, Dimitri Kharine or Kevin Hitchcock, all of whom were still on the Stamford Bridge professional playing staff.

And, indeed, he did that by making his Chelsea debut in the FA Charity Shield at Wembley against Manchester United.

To begin with, life in the Premiership was not easy for him although he confided, "To be honest I thought it would be even harder to settle in. It is more difficult in England and more physical. I took some games to get used to it and then it got better all the time."

And certainly his form in the second half of his first season was outstanding as the fans adopted him as one of their own, singing out his name over and again.

Kharine returned briefly, and both he and Hitchcock made isolated appearances. But the Dutchman was laying a permanent claim to his position, despite some unjustified criticism from sections of the press.

Having learned his 'English grammar', he was well prepared for his second season. Above all he realised that he had to toughen up.

Not that he had much to prove. Already he had established a Chelsea record for keeping the highest number of clean sheets in a season, beating Peter Bonetti's 26. He also made more appearances in a season than anyone had done previously (59), as well as the least goals conceded in any season in the top division.

And above all, he had the ideal temperament. Any soft goals given away (and they were very few) never allowed his confidence to be undermined. Equally important, he possessed the flair of making vital saves at crucial moments in a game.

Also, he simply relished the challenge of European club football. At the top of the list he put the brilliant saves against Real Betis, and an equally crucial series of heroics in the Vicenza games (especially in the last minute of the match at Stamford Bridge). And then there was equally vital rescues in the Final against Stuttgart in Stockholm.

It was on Boxing Day 2000, in the away Premiership fixture against Ipswich Town, that an unfortunate and uncharacteristic slip allowed the home team to fight back and equalise after Chelsea had set up a 2-0 lead.

Ed was clearly out of sorts and only a clearance off the line by John Terry in the final minute of the game enabled Chelsea to escape with a point.

And so in the next fixture, against Aston Villa on New Year's Day, Carlo Cudicini was preferred and immediately showed such excellent form that he permanently relegated the Dutchman on to the sidelines.

At the age of 34, and thoroughly integrated into English life in the Home Counties, he was ready to answer recalls into the senior side, **which came on three later occasions before reluctantly leaving** The Bridge in the summer of 2003, when he performed to his old high standard.

He may well ultimately turn to coaching and, with that in sight, he passed on his knowledge in sessions with young 'keepers on the club's books.

Chelsea Career
178-1 appearances

John Dempsey – not always in the limelight

PERHAPS as a result of being a member of Chelsea's most successful, and most star-studded line-up to that time, John Dempsey did not always receive the acclaim or the limelight which he deserved.

A true Londoner, he was born in Hampstead and played almost all his football in the capital. He signed apprentice forms for Fulham at the age of 16, turning professional two years later.

His build, standing 6ft 1in and turning the scales at around 13½st, suggested a defender. Yet in his first full season in the senior side at Craven Cottage he had a spell at centre-forward for six weeks or so, once scoring a hat-trick against Northampton Town in a Cup-tie.

Already, or so it seemed, part of the furniture at Fulham, it was therefore a surprise when he was transferred to Chelsea in January 1969 for a £70,000 fee.

Within weeks, and involving a reshuffling of the defence, he had taken over the centre-half berth he was to retain for the next three seasons and which included the winning of both the FA Cup (1970) and the European Cup-winners' Cup (1971).

And in each of those Finals he played a major role. At Wembley, in the first game against Leeds United, he held the rearguard together at a crucial time when Chelsea's right-hand flank was being cruelly exposed by Leeds' left wing.

Then, in the replay, not only did he dominate the defence in front of Peter Bonetti (whose mobility had been reduced by injury), but he also found time to move forward and almost score a crucial goal with a long-range dipping shot which only narrowly missed its target.

Equally important, John Dempsey occupied centre stage 12 months later in the European Cup winners' Cup Final (which again required two games) against Real Madrid in Athens.

In the first game he became the villain of the piece when an unfortunate miskick allowed an opposing defender to claim an equalising goal with only seconds of the match remaining.

Two days later, in the replay, he captured the headlines in rather different way by fastening on to a weak punch-out from the Madrid goalkeeper and hitting a stunning shot into the roof of the net.

It was without doubt the most valuable of his seven goals for Chelsea in over 200 appearances. And, not surprisingly, Dempsey enjoyed it too. "It was the biggest thrill of my career. I've never felt better than at that moment."

But it is, of course, as a powerful, and utterly reliable, defender that he will always be remembered.

He represented the Republic of Ireland on 19 occasions (made eligible for that country on account of his parents' birth qualifications). Above all he had an air of calm authority which he added to any defence of which he was a member, and which infected those around him.

Others in Chelsea's two Cup-winning sides of 1970 and 1971 may have captured a greater share of the limelight. None, though, played a more crucial role.

Chelsea Career

200-7 appearances   7 goals

Marcel Desailly – seeking a new emotion

HAS any player ever arrived at Stamford Bridge with greater pedigree, apart from possibly Ruud Gullitt? Or been greeted with greater expectation?

Marcel Desailly had already represented France on 49 occasions and played in a World Cup winning team in 1998 (when they beat Brazil 3-0 in a disappointing Final), won the French League championship, the European Cup (with Marseille twice), the European Super Cup, and two Italian League championships (with AC Milan).

And yet, at the age of 30, he came with burning ambition unabated and still with the ability to walk into any football club in the world. But why Chelsea?

"I wanted to come for the language, for the experience in England, and to know the Premier League championship."

He had experienced two indifferent seasons with AC Milan, and Chelsea manager Gianluca Vialli was keen to bring him to Stamford Bridge.

"It was not because of the money. The thing was I wanted myself new emotion," he explained.

Frank Leboeuf entered the equation, too, by recommending Chelsea. The size of the club was not a factor – rather their objectives. He realised that he also needed new motivation.

There was no settling-in period required. Whether at the heart of the defence, the territory which he knew best, or as an anchor midfield man, his superb technique enabled him to take everything in that big stride. So much at home was he, and so settled at Chelsea, that he signed a new contract in the summer of 2000, tying himself to the club until 2004 so that the Premiership championship could remain in his sights.

For years he has been the best centre-half in the world, His superb reading of the game carried his giant frame into the right spot and at the crucial time. He is athletic. He has pace. And once on the ball, he releases it only at his own inclination, and only then with such perfect accuracy.

Light years away from the perception of the traditional centre-half, his five years as a centre midfield operator with AC was a crucial part of his development into an all-rounder.

He is, too, his own most severe critic. An unenforced error irritates him more than his colleagues, or the fans. A misplaced pass against FC Copenhagen in the first leg of a Cup-winners' Cup-tie at the Bridge helped to give away a goal. But, he atoned by scoring the equaliser himself. It was a typical response.

Nowadays his international ambitions, already of course realised, take second place to those at Chelsea. Succeeding Dennis Wise in the captaincy role at the club was his latest challenge.

Even if signs that wear and tear after an already long career are showing (a persistent and recurring ankle injury has troubled him at times) there is no question of his sights being lowered.

If there proves to be no further peaks to scale, he will have left his mark on those around him such, as William Gallas and John Terry. It is already a lasting legacy.

Chelsea Career

195-2 appearances   7 goals

Roberto Di Matteo – inventing the game

FEW players from European football settled more immediately into the British game than Roberto Di Matteo.

Probably it helped that his expected role at Stamford Bridge was the same as it had been in Italy with Lazio where, despite their wealth of talent, the team had failed to win major honours.

Roberto was a highly talented creative midfield player and, as he once said, such men 'invent the game'.

Behind a handsome face was concealed a determination and tough approach, perhaps sharpened by his experiencing reputedly the hardest of all derby encounters, that between Lazio and AC Milan.

Chelsea's record signing up to that time – at £4.9 million – proved a wonderful investment. Amazingly Roberto was the first major current international to arrive at Stamford Bridge for 40 years. And manager Ruud Gullit knew that he was to prove an integral part of his ambitions to establish the club in the top bracket of Premiership clubs.

After almost being responsible for conceding a first-minute goal in his opening League fixture, at Southampton, Roberto, the anchor midfield and flanked by Craig Burley and Dennis Wise, settled easily into the side.

One week later he gave notice of what the Stamford Bridge fans could expect by scoring the only goal of the game with a 25-yard drive, five minutes from time.

And this was to prove one of his strengths and one with which he had not been notably linked previously. In the 1993 season in Switzerland, playing for the champions, Aarau, he managed only six goals but, nevertheless, was that country's Player of the Year.

Undoubtedly the goal for which he will be best remembered is his 43-second strike in the 1997 FA Cup Final at Wembley. Picking up a pass inside his own half of the field, he embarked on a 30-yard dash before unleashing an unstoppable shot from similar range, the ball flying into the net over the head of the bewildered Middlesbrough goalkeeper.

That was his ninth goal of the season, a total he bettered the following year when he found the target on 10 occasions. He again scored at Wembley, also against Middlesbrough, this time in the Coca-Cola Cup Final, albeit in less spectacular fashion as he connected with Zola's mishit corner. Seven weeks layer he added more silverware to his collection as Chelsea won the European Cup-winners' Cup in Stockholm.

In the autumn of 1999, his second manager at Chelsea, Gianluca Vialli, saw fit to change Roberto's role to fit into a more solid midfield to accommodate the arrival of Didier Deschamps and the emerging Jody Morris. A nine-week absence necessitated by ankle surgery also kept him out of first-team action. But yet again he scored at Wembley, in the 2000 FA Cup Final against Aston Villa. Chelsea won a dour game 1-0.

Worse still was to follow early in the next season when he suffered a broken leg in Chelsea's UEFA Cup-tie against St Gallon in Zurich. An anticipated 10-week lay-off proved sadly both inaccurate and optimistic and, in March 2002, Roberto Di Matteo was forced to announce his retirement at the age of 31.

He played an important part in two FA Cup victories, the UEFA Super Cup win, as well as successes in the European Cup-winners' and Football League Cups and an FA Charity shield success.

His name is firmly implanted in CFC history, both as an outstanding player and a most personable man.

Chelsea Career

155-20 appearances   26 goals

Kerry Dixon – scorer with a sound pedigree

FEW other clubs in the Football League can boast a more distinguished line of high-scoring centre-forwards than Chelsea, starting, of course, with George Hilsdon (82 goals in his first three seasons at Stamford Bridge) and continuing with Jimmy Floyd Hasselbaink almost a century later.

Claiming his spot in this distinguished line is Kerry Dixon (193 goals from 420 games), a total bettered only by Bobby Tambling.

It was manager John Neal in his reign as Chelsea's manager between 1981 and 1985 who signed Dixon from Reading for £165,000. Several other top clubs had hesitated. Neal pounced.

Dixon came with a sound pedigree – his father had scored goals for both Luton Town and Coventry City as well as in minor football.

Kerry had figured briefly at Tottenham Hotspur before being shipped off into non-League football with Chesham United and Dunstable Town where he first attracted the attention of Reading.

With the Berkshire club he scored 56 times in 116 League games, often with the style and panache he was to bring into the top flight. Yet still for some unexplained reason managers held back.

Two goals on his Chelsea debut, against Derby County on the opening day of the 1983–84 season, banished any doubts and from that moment on he never looked back.

Fortunate to link Dixon up with a kindred soul in David Speedie, the fiery terrier-like Scotsman, the club won the Second Division championship in the pair's first season in harness.

While the England selectors initially held back, Dixon continued to score prolifically, keeping Bobby Tambling's all-time Chelsea record in his sights and only narrowing missing that target, finishing nine goals short of Tambling's 202.

Some critics picked holes in Dixon's technique. Yet his four goals from eight England appearances (three after being summoned off the bench) would certainly be welcomed nowadays.

Six feet in height, Kerry was a natural athlete. Weighing 13st, he was well-equipped to withstand physical challenges. He was a fine header and, like Tommy Lawton almost 40 years earlier, could direct the ball past the goalkeeper with pin-point accuracy. His comparative weakness was a sometimes unpredictable first-touch.

A turning point in his career came when he suffered injury in an FA Cup-tie against Liverpool in January 1986, after which there was a feeling that he was never quite the same force again. His pace and acceleration dropped, as did his output of goals.

So, in July 1992, he moved off to Southampton, rejoining his old partner, David Speedie. But a lot of the magic had disappeared and at The Dell and, again, briefly with Luton Town, the old fires could not be ignited, although for a short time he became a provider of chances for others rather than being the executioner of old.

Once more his path crossed that of Chelsea, when he turned out for Luton Town against some of his former colleagues in the FA Cup semi-final at Wembley in 1994. He was warmly acclaimed by his old Stamford Bridge worshippers even if no longer occupying his blue shirt. In fact, a goal would have probably been greeted as if the clock had been turned back.

Chelsea Career

413-17 appearances   193 goals

Tommy Docherty – no more colourful character

IN the autumn of 1961 Ted Drake was beginning his tenth season as manager of Chelsea Football Club. Having rebuilt the playing staff at minimum cost to his directors, and brought the Football League championship to Stamford Bridge after half a century of frustration and failure, it was clear that major surgery was once again required if the club was to progress.

Age had taken its toll and Drake's recent signings had fallen short of expectation.

It came as no surprise, therefore, when just over three weeks into the new season, with Chelsea floundering in the lower reaches of the First Division table, a new coach was appointed.

The person involved, on the other hand, did arouse comment and no little excitement.

'Arsenal, in order to help us in our present difficulties, have agreed to let us sign Tommy Docherty as a player... such an experienced player cannot help but be an asset to our present team of youngsters,' was the official statement.

In fact Tommy Docherty, at the age of 33, turned out in the next four League games before retiring as a player to concentrate on coaching duties. Then, one month later, Ted Drake was dismissed.

The new chief coach was not appointed to the rank of team manager until the following February, but he soon realised that, with little cash available for new signings, he would largely have to rely on his squad of promising youngsters. Sadly, Docherty had arrived too late on the scene to persuade Jimmy Greaves to stay at the Bridge, although he was convinced that if he, rather than the club secretary, had been allowed to conduct the transfer negotiations he could have persuaded the little genius to sign for him.

After graduating to the title of manager, Docherty lost eight of his first ten games in charge, and some time before the end of the season relegation became a virtual certainty.

But it proved something of a blessing in disguise. Out went four senior players, and the 1962–63 season began with eight 19-year-olds under the captaincy of Bobby Tambling (20). And Chelsea, after losing their momentum following a two-month interruption caused by a prolonged winter freeze, achieved promotion on the final day of the season.

That was merely the prelude for what was to follow. Chelsea's chairman of those days, Joe Mears, who was also the highly respected chairman of the Football Association, was an ideal foil. Above all, Tommy Docherty held his chief in high regard. And, for his part, Mears was a wise counsellor and, at times, a restraining influence on some of Docherty's more impetuous deeds and ideas.

As Tommy put it; "He was more like a father to us and was always available to myself and the players, even when I, or one of the lads, was in trouble... and whatever decision he made, it was respected."

In partnership they took the club forward to success which Chelsea had not previously attained in more than 60 years of endeavour.

Following promotion, positions of fifth, third and ninth was a new experience. And, in May 1967, Chelsea reached the FA Cup Final for only the second time in their history, 12 months after appearing in the Inter-Cities' Fairs Cup semi-final against Barcelona. The future held promise of further exciting progress, but for Docherty it was not to be.

On 1 July 1966, Joe Mears collapsed and died during the World Cup finals in England; his successor, Charles Pratt, was never on the same wavelength with Tommy Docherty who had sadly lost his sage and mentor.

Incidents on Chelsea's 1967 summer tour of Bermuda precipitated a crisis, unravelling by the day. As a result, Docherty resigned on 6 October 1967 and an exciting and successful era in the Chelsea story was at an end.

However, he had left behind a generous legacy on the playing staff which enabled his successor, Dave Sexton, to carry forward the club on to their Cup-winning deeds of 1970 and 1971.

But, 15 years later, in October 1981, Tommy Docherty reflected ruefully,"If Joe Mears had not died and instead continued at the helm of Stamford Bridge. I would still be Chelsea's manager to this day." As it is, The Doc can look back on a managerial career which has taken in a variety of posts since Chelsea. Never has the label 'much-travelled manager' been so appropriately attached.

Chelsea Career

4 appearances

Ted Drake – the happiest day of his life

WHEN Ted Drake strode purposefully into Stamford Bridge in the summer of 1952 he left no one in any doubt that he was determined to change the whole image of Chelsea Football Club and leave no stone unturned until he had abolished nearly half a century of underachievement and put some meaningful silverware into the trophy cabinet.

"I have felt that the club deserved to do itself fuller justice than ever it has done in the past. It is my job to see this greater standing is forthcoming, and foremost in the making of the successful Chelsea we all want to see must be the atmosphere of one big happy family linking directors, players, staff and you, the paying public."

And Drake could speak from experience. As a player with Arsenal he had won two League championships and the FA Cup, with the club never once during his half a dozen seasons at Highbury finishing outside the top six in the old First Division.

Further, his 182 first-team appearances had brought him 138 goals, a remarkable strike rate.

All was not immediately plain sailing in the Fulham Road and the task ahead of him was even more daunting than he had anticipated. In fact a 3-1 victory over Manchester City at Stamford Bridge on the last day of his first season was only just enough to stave off relegation and bring to an end "weeks of great mental strain for our players and officials".

But his influx of players from the lower divisions, whom had seen during his first managerial appointment at Reading, swiftly brought dividends; the likes of Stan Willemse and John McNichol (from Brighton & Hove Albion), Frank Blunstone (Crewe Alexandra) and Stan Wicks (his captain at Elm Park) were men of strong character as well as proven ability, and provided a framework for Chelsea's 1955 Football League championship side.

Three amateurs also made the step-up easily and with great success.

So, after some 33 months following his first public pronouncement, he had achieved his aim. The image of the Chelsea Pensioner had for ever been banished on that unforgettable day of 23 April 1955, as Sheffield Wednesday were beaten 3-0 in front of 51,000 supporters rejoicing in an occasion most never thought they would live to see – the Football League championship at last!

Drake certainly had not left any stone unturned as he emotionally addressed the crowd swarming in front of the main stand.

"This is the happiest moment of my life. At the start of the season I was asked if we would win the Cup. I thought we might but I thought we had a greater chance of winning the championship. I congratulate all the boys and everyone of the staff, office, training and playing. Right through they are one and all Chelsea."

As he had set out to do almost three years before, he truly had created the 'atmosphere of one big happy family'.

Undoubtedly he must have realised time was running against him. The core of his first team, even with the new recruits, were in the autumn of their footballing careers. And major rebuilding was on the agenda.

Sadly, with financial constraints this proved too high a hurdle to surmount and, at the age of 49, Ted Drake retired from the game altogether.

But his name remains large in Chelsea FC's history as others strive to equal his cherished achievement on that sunny afternoon half a century ago.

Ted Drake died in May 1995, at Raynes Park, Surrey.

Micky Droy – a major feature at the Bridge

THE name of Micky Droy is part of the folklore of Chelsea Football Club. For more than a dozen years he was a major feature of the Stamford Bridge scene.

Unfortunately, like several of his generation, his career coincided with probably the most difficult years of all in Chelsea's history. Financial problems had escalated; the future of Stamford Bridge was uncertain; and the team was short of the quality that it was not to acquire for another decade or more.

Micky Droy's first-team career at Chelsea spanned 15 seasons. He made his debut in February 1971 when the team was on course for its European Cup-winners' Cup triumph over Real Madrid in Athens (Micky appearing in one of the semi-final legs), and his last appearance was 14 years later, in February 1985 when he returned, briefly, after a long period of absence through injury.

Originally competition for his position in the side was intense, from such as John Dempsey, David Webb and Marvin Hinton. But he outfought them all to become part of the senior team's furniture.

At 6ft 4in Micky was one of the tallest players in the history of Chelsea FC. Not surprisingly, his complete aerial domination in the centre of the defence was his hallmark. On the ground he preferred to play the ball on his left side, cleverly disguising his weakness on the right. His range in the tackle was increased by his left foot frequently lunging out like an extending telescope dispossessing unwary attackers.

Although his footwork was surprisingly dainty for such a big man and, on occasions, would draw loud applause when produced almost like a conjuror's trick, it must be admitted that he was a little short of the finer skills of the game at ground level.

Nevertheless, when open space in front of him allowed, he would power forward with gathering acceleration to the accompaniment of roars of approval from supporters.

And he took his role when captaining the side very seriously. He was a leader who inspired those around him and who demanded high standards. He was a good organiser of his defence.

During his long reign at Stamford Bridge, as well as experiencing the thrill of European competition, and promotion in 1977, his final season game was in the top flight in 1985 after another promotion year in 1983–84 when he had been absent through injury.

And he had been at his post at Bolton, in May 1983, when relegation to Division Three was averted by the narrowest of margins.

Then, with his 34th birthday looming, his Chelsea days came to an end. He had borne the heat and burden of many days and with such as Joe McLaughin (21) and Colin Pates (20) emerging from the wings, it was time to leave despite Micky Droy's own reluctance.

He had always had an ambition to move on to the coaching staff. But that was not to be and he still had the urge to continue as player.

So Crystal Palace signed him and he was there for 18 months (56 first-team games) and then Brentford found a place for him for a short time.

But Chelsea had always been his club.

Chelsea Career

302-11 appearances   19 goals

Paul Elliott – a footballing tragedy

INEVITABLY in the life of any football club whose history spans almost 100 years, there will be times of darkness as well as light; tragedy as well as joy. And there is no more tragic story in Chelsea's history than that surrounding Paul Elliott.

Signed from Celtic in July 1991 for a fee of £1.4 million, and already skipper of the England 'B' team, he arrived in the Fulham Road with burning enthusiasm.

Aged 27, he had already played for Charlton Athletic, Luton Town and Pisa, as well as Celtic.

"Chelsea have convinced me how ambitious they are and now I feel I have a platform to pursue my own England ambitions," he announced on his arrival at Stamford Bridge.

And his impact was immediate. At the end of his first-season at his new club he was Player of the Year and was described by one rival manager as 'the best aerial person in the League'.

As well as showing himself to be a brilliant defender he was a superb organiser of his colleagues. It was planned that he would be the lynchpin around which manager Ian Porterfield would take his side forward.

But it was not to be. On Saturday, 5 September 1992, against Liverpool at Anfield, 10 minutes into the game, a tackle from Dean Saunders inflicted an horrific injury from which Elliott never recovered despite receiving the best possible medical treatment and his own long hours conscientiously carrying out the expert and specialised advice he had been given.

And so his football, and his Chelsea career, was cut off at the age of 28 when his ambition was firmly focussed on receiving full international recognition, as well as leading Chelsea to further honours.

In his brief time at Stamford Bridge he had much to look back on. The FA Cup run to the quarter-final in March 1992. An early season 3-1 victory over Tottenham Hotspur at White Hart Lane, erasing the humiliation experienced by a resounding 3-0 defeat against Oldham Athletic three days earlier. And a welcome home victory in the League against Nottingham Forest when Chelsea played 'keep-ball' for about a minute and a half at the end of the contest.

Later, however, faced with the inevitable, he announced his retirement the weekend before the 1994 FA Cup Final.

At the reception on the Saturday evening he received a standing ovation from 400 people which lasted well over a minute. In an electrically emotional weekend it was perhaps the most testing moment of all.

Soon after the court case against the Liverpool player involved in his injury was heard and he was able to look back upon his all-too-brief time at the Bridge, he summed up his feelings

"I had known for the last four months that I wasn't making as much progress as I wanted. For all my honourable intentions my knee couldn't perform its duties.

"Physically I was in the best shape of my life. I worked very hard. Mentally I was so positive. But the extent of the injury proved very difficult. That was the hardest to accept."

When the surgeon gave Paul the final verdict, he asked him to repeat what he had said. And the specialist added that it was probably the worst football injury he had ever seen. The damage to the cruciate ligaments of one knee were irreparable.

Through all his tribulations he had many to whom he was grateful at Chelsea: the chairman, Bob Ward (the then physiotherapist); Glenn Hoddle (after he arrived as manager); and his Mum.

"Rest assured," he said, "I'm a life-long Chelsea supporter."

Chelsea Career

55 appearances   3 goals

Harry Ford – every manager would like one

HARRY Ford was the type of player every manager likes to have on the payroll, in that he would always be ready to answer to any emergency and play wherever, and whenever the situation demanded.

To call him a 'utility' player, however, would be a grave injustice, despite his reputation for versatility.

Basically he was a right winger and ideally suited for that role. Small of stature (5ft 7½in) he was extremely fast and would tantalise an opponent with delicate footwork before leaving the defender trailing in his wake.

Not the least of his talents was the accuracy of his crosses and providing goalscoring opportunities for the Chelsea centre-forwards of his day. Nor was his own marksmanship to be despised as his tally of almost 50 goals proves.

But for the four seasons lost to World War One, Harry Ford would almost certainly have established a record for most first-team appearances.

As it was he played almost 250 games spread over 11 years from 1912 to 1923.

It was in the season leading up to the outbreak of the war that he reached his peak and made a major contribution to steering Chelsea to their first-ever FA Cup Final, against Sheffield United at Old Trafford.

In the first round of that 1914-15 season, against Swindon Town, he scored a vital equalising goal in the replay three minutes before the end of full-time, after the first game had resulted in a 1-1 draw.

Not only did that save Chelsea's bacon but it provided the launching pad for a 5-2 win in extra-time.

Equally crucial was his goal in the fourth Cup-tie, a replay against Newcastle United at St James's Park.

The Final, sadly, was a game easily forgotten so far as the quality of football produced. And most especially for Harry.

Early in the match, in an accidental collision, he was dazed and played the rest of the contest scarcely aware of what was going on around him. And, of course, there were no substitutes in those days.

Playing intermittently throughout the war, Harry resumed in his usual spot in the autumn of 1919, still only 26. And for five more seasons he plied his trade down the right flank he had made his own, and even on occasions moving into an inside position.

Although Ford was born in Fulham, Chelsea had spotted him playing for Tunbridge Wells Rangers, his only other club. At the age of 31 he decided to call it a day with Chelsea.

A straightforward honest-to-goodness trier, Harry never picked up any representative honours. Chelsea was his life and his days at the Bridge were happy and contented.

There have been few more faithful Chelsea servants down the years.

Chelsea Career

248 appearances   46 goals

Dick Foss – what price his protégés?

LOOKING through any table of Chelsea players' statistics, the name of Dick Foss would scarcely attract a second glance.

Born in Barking, he was playing amateur football for Southall in 1936 when he was brought to the attention of Chelsea.

Already aged 24, it was perhaps surprising that he had remained unnoticed by London's professional clubs for so long.

Having spent the first six months or so of his first season at Stamford Bridge playing in the Combination team, mostly at inside-left, he had made little apparent impact. Then, in February 1937, he made his first-team debut, against Sheffield Wednesday at Hillsborough, where Chelsea emerged with a creditable 1-1 draw.

Following that, he retained his position for the next three games.

In fact that position was awaiting a successor to the ageing George Gibson but the problem was temporarily solved by switching Harry Burgess to that side of the attack.

However, twice more before the outbreak of World War Two, Foss was given an extended trial, but it never seemed likely that he was to stake a permanent claim to a place in the League side.

Working in London during the war provided the opening he was seeking at a time when clubs were desperately trying to complete their line-ups week by week. As a member of an almost regular 'Russell-Harris-Foss' half-back line, he played some 200 games. Even so, when normal football resumed in the autumn of 1946, he found his place, either at wing-half or inside-forward, usually usurped by big-money signings, and notably by England's Len Goulden.

However, in 1952 he was appointed manager of the Chelsea youth scheme and for the next 14 years he was responsible for producing the most prodigious line of talent any club had known up to that time.

Today, what would be the combined values of such as Bobby Smith, Jimmy Greaves, Peter Brabrook, Barry Bridges, Ken Shellito, Peter Bonetti, John Hollins, Alan Hudson, Peter Osgood (England internationals all and amassing almost 50 caps)? All emerged from Dick's production line.

And during that period, in 1960 and 1961, Chelsea won the FA Youth Cup for the only times.

Bracketed with Dick should be scout Jimmy Thompson (himself a Chelsea player in the late 1920s). Jimmy was the producer. Dick was the polisher.

After 30 years, Foss left Stamford Bridge, and retired from football altogether.

Before his death a few years ago, he was interviewed and asked two questions, above all others.

His biggest disappointment? Missing the game against Moscow Dynamo in November 1945 after picking up an injury three days previously.

The best player to emerge from the juniors during his time as youth coach? Jimmy Greaves.

So the 46 peacetime first-team appearances spanning 11 years are an irrelevant sideshow so far as Dick Foss is concerned.

Rather, his value to Chelsea FC should be trying to tot up the price of what his protégés would have fetched in today's transfer market.

Chelsea Career

48 appearances   3 goals

Willie Foulke – a giant of a goalkeeper

WATCHING the lithe, athletic, Carlo Cudicini keeping goal for Chelsea in the 21st century is a reminder of how far the game has changed since the club's beginning in 1905.

When the team stepped out to fulfil their first competitive fixture almost 100 years ago, their goalkeeper was William Henry Foulke, who had been secured from Sheffield United for a fee of £50.

Aged 29 he was, standing 6ft 3in and weighing 22st, already a legend. As one writer put it, 'Chelsea didn't just dress the shop window to get themselves into the Football League, they filled it with Billy Foulke.'

Many are the amusing tales, some embroidered maybe, about the big man. But he was one of the best goalkeepers of his day and good enough to have kept goal for England against Wales in 1897.

He may have been a joke to many. But certainly not to opponents trying to put the ball past him.

Picking up the ball in one hand, he would initiate attacks with giant, long-distance throws, his fisting away from corner kicks often enabled the ball to reach the halfway line.

The 35 competitive games in his one season at Stamford Bridge contained 17 clean sheets (nine of them in consecutive games).

John Tait Robertson, his manager at Stamford Bridge, summed up the value of the man as 'a draw alone he is worth his weight in gold; his astonishing ability has aroused a fever of interest in his doings beneath the bar for Chelsea'.

Then, of course, were the many tales of Willie which have passed into legend.

On arrival at a northern railway station he became detached from the rest of the Chelsea team and was turned back by the ticket collectors at the barrier who, not surprisingly, refused to believe he was a member of the football party. Whereupon, he picked two of them up, one under each arm, and carried them struggling and protesting into the ticket master's office.

With Sheffield United, in a semi-final Cup-tie, he had become irritated by the Liverpool centre-forward, eventually grabbing his opponent by the ankles and standing him upside down with his head in the thick mud.

Liverpool, as a result, were awarded a penalty-kick from which they scored the only goal of the game.

Willie was particularly famous himself for saving penalties. In a Chelsea fixture, against Burton United, he saved two such kicks from the same player, causing the poor man to attract abuse and criticism from his colleagues.

"Why did you shoot straight at him?" "I had to," the forward replied, "there was no room on either side!"

Chelsea loved him, and he loved life in London, and added a further two stones to his weight in his short time at Stamford Bridge before returning north to sign for Bradford City.

After retiring, he set up a stall on the sands at Blackpool beach, establishing a penalty-kick business. A penny a time to try to score past the giant, and threepence reward for each successful attempt.

It was this venture which caused his end when, having caught a chill, he died at the age of 42.

Apart from his one international cap, he won FA Cup winners' medals in 1899 and 1902 with Sheffield United, and a losers' medal in 1901. And it was with the Bramall Lane club that he scored the only goal of his career in open play.

A unique personality, his surname at birth was registered as 'Foulk', at death as 'Foulkes'. An all-round cricketer, he played four first-class matches for Derbyshire, once scoring a half-century against Essex at Leyton before being stumped.

Chelsea Career

35 appearances

Hughie Gallacher – the flawed genius

TO say that Hughie Gallacher was a law unto himself and, some would say, the greatest of all centre-forwards down the years may sound an outrageous claim but those who knew him, and saw him play, have few doubts on the matter.

He had his own ideas and stuck unwaveringly to them.

Standing 5ft 5in in height and weighing under 11st, he was scarcely built to play in this position, let alone to become the best of his era.

Born in Bellshill, Lanarkshire, in 1903, he started in local football before signing for Queen of the South Wanderers and then Airdrieonians before coming to England in December 1925 with Newcastle United, following long drawn-out negotiations for a fee which was never made public.

His first nine games in the Football League brought 15 goals and the Geordies had immediately taken the little man to their hearts.

By then, of course, he was established in the Scottish national side, having made his debut soon after his 21st birthday, and went on to win 20 caps at a time when three international fixtures a season was the normal quota.

On Tyneside he was worshipped and he captained Newcastle to the Football League championship in 1926–27 and was one of his country's 'Wembley Wizards' in March 1928, when the Scots put five goals past England.

Leaving Newcastle United seemed unthinkable and Chelsea's initial overtures in May 1930 were not well received either by Hughie or, of course, his vast army of admirers.

However a transfer fee of £10,000 had been agreed and, apparently no longer wanted, he felt bound to move on. In fact it was rumoured that the player's extravagant nightlife was not to Newcastle's liking.

At Stamford Bridge he was quickly made to feel at home with such fellow Scottish internationals as Andy Wilson and Tommy Law. But digs in Barons Court were far removed from anything he had known before.

Primarily, of course, Hughie wanted the ball played on the ground. He was adept in bringing colleagues into his web with '1-2' passing movements, and his shooting was a deadly weapon, simple and accurate placement past the opposing goalkeeper ending many a build up.

Often, though, he was his own worst enemy. He attracted rough treatment – physical and verbal – from the opposition well aware that Gallacher's hot temper could easily be brought to boiling point (on one occasion he, wisely, asked the referee's permission to briefly leave the field to calm down!)

Especially keen were his duels with Arsenal's powerful centre-half of those days, Herbie Roberts, 'the policeman'. But four goals in such battles suggest that the little man gave as good as he got.

Gallacher's departure to Derby County in November 1934 came as a shock. But at the age of 31, and with his lifestyle and attachment to the demon drink combined with marital problems, probably meant that it was for the best. He was heavily in debt too, after a divorce.

But 81 goals from 144 games speaks for itself and he left behind an indelible memory of his marvellous skills and his showmanship.

In the short term Hughie's move to Derby was a great success. He fitted into a talented side and it almost resulted in another championship medal coming his way.

Later his career wound down with Notts County, Grimsby Town and Gateshead, in 1938–39, where he was still scoring goals regularly (18 from 31 games). After one or two wartime appearances, he called it a day.

Tragically, Hughie's life ended in the saddest possible manner.

Alcohol proved his greatest enemy to the very end. In May 1957 his son was taken into care following complaints that Gallagher had assaulted the boy whom he idolised.

Unable to face the inevitable publicity, he threw himself on to a railway line and was killed instantly by an oncoming train.

Chelsea Career

144 appearances   81 goals

Len Goulden – one of the greatest of his time

LOOKING back, it is hard to realise that Len Goulden was a Chelsea first-team player for only four seasons – so great an impression did he make.

Without question he was one of the greatest inside-forwards of his time.

For two years before World War Two he was England's first choice inside-left; this whilst playing for West Ham United, then a middle-of-the-table Second Division side.

Particularly he was remembered for his skill and craftsmanship in England's 6-3 win in Germany, and an equally impressive role in his country's victory over Scotland at Hampden Park in 1939.

Goulden had won 14 caps for his country before the outbreak of World War Two and played in another half-dozen wartime internationals. But for the seven-year gap caused by hostilities, his impact on English football would have been immeasurably greater still.

Signing for Chelsea in August 1945, for a £4,500 fee, was a wonderful bargain.

Probably he is best recalled for the role in the now legendary FA Cup semi-finals in 1950 against Arsenal.

Then past his 37th birthday and his first-class career apparently over (he was then mainly involved in coaching the Reserves), he was dramatically summoned back due to an injury to Bobby Campbell.

Hastily preparing himself with a punishing fitness training programme, and with only one Football Combination game, he simply rolled back the years and, as Chelsea's skipper said afterwards, "Len played as well as I've ever seen him play."

That match ended in a draw and, despite his contribution, great persuasion was required before he would agree to turn out in the replay.

He was never a prolific scorer of goals although he did net 70 from some 350 Football League outings.

"It is my job to make goals for others," he once said. And this he achieved superbly well with consummate skill.

He would draw defenders, like moths to a lamp, and then effortlessly weave his way past them with a kick or a swerve in a crowded area.

He stood 5ft 8in and his magic feet were the foundation of his success. He invariably played the ball on the ground and insisted others should do likewise.

It is perhaps interesting to speculate on how he would have fared in the present-day game. Goulden was a dictator in the middle of the field, slowing the pace to his liking. As a result, errors and inaccuracies were eliminated, or at least kept to a minimum.

After his playing days were finally over, he remained on the Stamford Bridge coaching staff for a period, turning down an offer to manage Chelmsford City before taking over that role at Watford, followed by spells at Banbury United and Oxford United.

In this field he did not achieve the outstanding success he had reached as a player. Although possessing one of the most shrewd brains in football, perhaps he could not pass on his philosophy of the game to others.

Or maybe they could not master those skills in which he was supreme.

Chelsea Career

111 appearances   19 goals

Jimmy Greaves – the most remarkable goalscorer

THAT Jimmy Greaves is the most remarkable goalscorer in the history of British football is probably a fair claim. It is therefore all the more regrettable that Chelsea had only four seasons of the extraordinary little man's career.

For nearly a dozen seasons in English League football (punctuated by a brief spell in Italy) no opposing defence could stem his flood of goals, many of them from openings he himself had carved open.

From the moment his jaunty step brought him through the Stamford Bridge gates in 1955, the limelight and the sporting headlines focussed on this slip of a lad with a cheery smile and twinkle-toe feet.

Fourteen goals from 17 games with the juniors was a respectable start, but one which was dwarfed in his second season of 1956–57 when, in all matches, he totalled 114 – a feat for which he was presented with an illuminated address.

There seemed little point in wasting time in reserve-team football, and so he was thrown into the deep end and made his debut in the Football League on 24 August 1957, against Tottenham Hotspur at White Hart Lane. Almost inevitably, with five minutes remaining, he dribbled his way past several white shirts to salvage a point for Chelsea in a 1-1 draw.

Another five goals in the next eight games confirmed his promise, whereupon manager Ted Drake, protecting him from heavier grounds, rested him until November before producing him as a special present on Christmas Day. Only too happy again to stretch his legs he obliged by scoring four times in a 7-4 win against Portsmouth. From then on, and for the rest of his career in SW6, he was never again absent other than through injury.

And other memorable occasions followed. The subject of tight marking from Wolves' England internationals Billy Wright, Ron Flowers and Bill Slater, Greaves simply left them flat-footed and bewildered as he skated past, and around, them to score five goals in a humiliating 6-1 victory against arguably England's top team at that time.

Twice more he hit the target on five occasions in a game, and scored a century of goals in the top flight before his 21st birthday, a feat never before achieved.

Not that his talent and skills can be measured purely mathematically. First he relied on superb control allied to a balance which allowed him to change direction and 'wrong-foot' the opposition. His speed and acceleration left defenders standing and helpless.

His old-fashioned dribbling at deceptive speed would see him weaving his way through a defence before leaving the final execution of placing the ball into net, the simplest part of the whole thing.

So many are the memories of his Stamford Bridge days that it is difficult to conceive that they were all crammed into four seasons.

His final bow for Chelsea, in a First Division fixture at the Bridge, was another special Jimmy Greaves occasion.

In front of his own suspect defence he left the Nottingham Forest rearguard chaotic and in tatters as he scored four times to leave the stage for the last time, having steered Chelsea to a 4-3 victory.

With the maximum wage still in force in England, he was away to Italy with AC Milan before returning to Tottenham Hotspur (the hardest of all Jimmy's career movements for Chelsea fans to bear) where in eight seasons he totted up another 200 goals and more.

By then he had accumulated 57 international caps for England.

Aged 31, and following a serious illness a year or two earlier, he moved to West Ham United for one more complete season. However, despite holding a first-team place, much of the glamour and sparkle had evaporated.

A battle against alcoholism was won and he became equally well known as a TV pundit.

But no one could ever argue with the summary of the little genius, by Stan Cullis the famous England international and manager of Wolverhampton Wanderers.

"The greatest finisher of all time."

Chelsea Career

169 appearances   132 goals

Ron Greenwood – answered an SOS

BORN in Lancashire, near Burnley, from Chelsea's point of view, it was a fortunate break when Ron Greenwood emigrated to London at the age of 10 where his father was employed.

Football was in his blood ('a common language' as he once said) from his earliest days. Living within a mile or two of Wembley Stadium, he was soon made captain of his school XI and represented Wembley Boys at Under-14 and Under-15 levels, before going in to play a variety of local teams.

It was a defining moment in Greenwood's career, however, when in 1939 a Chelsea Youth XI came to play a London Minor Cup semi-final against his local club at the time, Alperton.

Remarkably, no fewer than nine members of that team so impressed that they were invited to Stamford Bridge for a trial and as a result young Greenwood, a centre-half, was invited to sign.

"Their tradition and style appealed to one and I knew that because of the war they were forming an Under-19 team; the start of the famous Chelsea Youth scheme."

Further promotion soon followed and, answering an SOS call, Ron was summoned from Fulham, where he was due to play for Chelsea Reserves, and thrust into the senior side to turn out against Aldershot who, in those days of wartime guest players, included an all-international half-back line.

"I won't claim that I had an outstanding game but I survived and we beat Aldershot 6-0." After that he was posted for military service to Northern Ireland (where he played for Belfast Celtic) before the war took him to France.

After demobilisation he found John Harris firmly established as Chelsea's centre-half and, with little chance of breaking into the first team, signed for Bradford (PA) where his family were living.

Two seasons at Park Avenue were followed by four at Brentford (142 League games) before the wheel turned the full circle.

Soon after arriving at Stamford Bridge as manager, Ted Drake signed Greenwood. "I felt I was coming home and I had the chance to show what I could do at the highest level, and went straight into the League side."

Playing in the top division for the first time posed no problem, although Drake's philosophy of the game did not always coincide with Greenwood's.

Still the manager knew his man and the outstanding qualities he brought into the team.

The 1954–55 season (Greenwood's third at Chelsea) was, of course, the club's famous Football League championship campaign.

Then aged 33, Greenwood was the undisputed first choice for the centre-half position until Christmas, but, waiting in the wings was one of Ted Drake's signings from Reading (where Drake had been manager), Stan Wicks.

Against Arsenal, at Highbury on Christmas Day, centre-forward Tommy Lawton scored the only goal of the game for the Gunners.

Twenty-four hours later the manager brought in Wicks for his Chelsea debut and Ron Greenwood never played in Chelsea's first team again.

A month or so later Fulham made an offer and Greenwood's 15-year interrupted association with Chelsea was over as he moved to Craven Cottage on a free transfer, Drake being honest enough to admit, "Obviously your future's not here now."

"I was sorry to leave Chelsea because they had always looked after me," Ron said years afterwards.

But all was not quite over as Ron Greenwood had played enough games to qualify for a Football League championship medal and quite rightly, was invited to the celebrations at Stamford Bridge at the end of the season.

Chelsea Career
66 appearances

Ruud Gullitt – the greatest all-rounder

FEW would argue that Ruud Gullitt was the greatest all-rounder ever to play for Chelsea.

Arriving on a free transfer from Sampdoria in June 1995, and approaching his 33rd birthday, many thought that his playing career was effectively over.

Certainly the former World Player of the Year, and twice Dutch Footballer of the Year, and the winner of 65 international caps for Holland and no fewer than 12 domestic Cup and League honours, had nothing more to prove.

But from his first day at Stamford Bridge he simply relished the new challenge and Glenn Hoddle was the right manager to give him his head.

He was signed to fulfil the sweeper role much favoured by Glenn. But returning after a six-week absence through injury in the first half of the season, he was pushed forward to play in central midfield for the only time in his career.

Down the years, from Vivian Woodward before World War One, via Hughie Gallacher, Greaves, Cooke and Osgood to Alan Hudson, Chelsea have possessed players of world class to attract the crowds down to the Fulham Road. But none could have claimed to exceed Ruud's quality on the ball.

And everything was accomplished with a grace and style which made it all appear ridiculously simple.

Then, in the summer of 1996, he was appointed Chelsea's manager after Glenn Hoddle had been tempted by the FA to take control of the national side. For Gullitt it was yet another challenge he was eager to grasp.

He made it clear that he did not wish to be regarded as a regular player, holding himself ready to fill a vacancy in the team as and when required. And, of course, his versatility meant that apart from keeping goal (one presumes!) he could perform with distinction anywhere on the park.

In fact, he made only a handful of further appearances (mostly as substitute). But by far his greatest contribution as manager was to entice some of football's top stars to the Bridge. Names which before he parted company with the club were already Chelsea legends in their own rights.

Gianluca Vialli and Gianfranco Zola may well have topped a group of the highest quality. But Roberto Di Matteo and Frank Leboeuf were little, if at all, outside that bracket.

Then, in the middle of February 1998, a bombshell exploded as Gullitt left Chelsea, protesting that he did not know the real reason.

In fact, he was seeking to sign a two-year player-coaching agreement, whereas the club had offered him a three-year coaching (only) contract which he had ignored for several months. Strangely, although he had played little first-team football for two years, that appetite still persisted, even though he seldom trained and was rarely on hand when he could have filled temporary gaps caused by injuries and suspensions. And his wage demands were certainly a further factor of dispute.

But everyone who had been connected with Chelsea Football Club during those brief, exciting times will recall the glamour, excitement and achievement Ruud brought with him.

Himself a world superstar, and inspired by his presence on and off the field, he lifted expectations at Chelsea as well as bringing a major trophy to Stamford Bridge when Chelsea won the FA Cup in 1997. And three months after his departure, of course, the European Cup-winners' Cup also came to Stamford Bridge.

He will never be forgotten during his, too-brief, stay.

Chelsea Career

50-14 appearances   7 goals

Harold Halse – a master of footwork

PLAYERS change clubs for all sorts of different reasons. Similarly managers are alerted to footballers' talents and potential in many, and often curious, ways.

In September 1908 the Football Association created a new trophy, the FA Charity Shield, and the early contests in that competition took place at Stamford Bridge. On Monday, 25 September 1911, the game was between Manchester United, the Football League champions, and Swindon Town, the Southern League champions.

Appearing at centre-forward for United was Harold Halse, aged 26, a Londoner who, after service with Clapton Orient and Southend United, had moved into top-class football three years earlier.

United won a highly entertaining match, 8-4, with their centre-forward, Halse, scoring six of the goals.

In fact he had played most of his career at inside-forward and had made a reputation as a regular scorer of goals (50 from 124 games in his Old Trafford career).

On that late summer's day in London he clearly made an indelible impression, although it would be another four years, after his new club, Aston Villa, placed Halse on the transfer list, before Chelsea could sign him.

It was fitting that Halse returned to London because he was a true Cockney, born in Leytonstone with whom he began his footballing career as an amateur.

With Manchester United he had partnered the legendary Billy Meredith and had won two Football League championship medals and an FA Cup medal.

A lightweight, Halse was 5ft 8in and weighed 10½st. His career up to that time had been laced with success; he had gained a third FA Cup winners' medal with Villa, on which occasion he was a central figure in a controversy.

In those days players did not carry numbers on their backs, making identification more difficult than in the present day.

Originally credited with the only goal in Villa's 1-0 victory, it was afterwards established he had been confused with the true scorer, one of his wing-half colleagues.

Halse was a clever ball-player, 'a master of footwork', as he was once described. He created openings for others and was himself a deadly marksman.

It was in the 1914–15 season that he reached his peak at Chelsea, playing in all eight games en route to the Cup Final.

Particularly remembered, and perhaps his best game with Chelsea, was in the second-round tie against Woolwich Arsenal at Stamford Bridge.

In a tense, dour struggle (Halse afterwards described it as the hardest game in which he had ever played) he received the ball inside his own half before embarking on a great run which he crowned by scoring the only goal of the match.

He played in every tie that season, also scoring Chelsea's first goal in the semi-final at Villa Park.

Occasionally he figured at centre-forward but he always said he was more suited to an inside position, providing scoring opportunities for others.

Well past the age of 30 when World War One ended, he played on for another season before winding down his Stamford Bridge career mainly at wing-half.

He then joined Charlton Athletic, playing on for two more seasons before retiring in the 1923 close season.

Chelsea Career

111 appearances   25 goals

John Harris – Chelsea's wartime gain

MORE than most areas of the country, London benefited from professional footballers from the north, midlands and beyond the Scottish border being stationed in the capital, or passing through en route to theatres of war abroad, from 1939-45.

And Chelsea profited better than almost any other club with such as George Hardwick (from Middlesbrough) Peter McKennan (Partick) and Charlie Mitten (Manchester United), but best of all the trio of Bobby Russell (Airdrieonians), Danny Winter (Bolton) and John Harris (Wolverhampton Wanderers), three who never returned home, throwing in their lot at Stamford Bridge.

And measured in length of service and appearances for the club, Harris was the most valuable import of all.

He had started his career with Swindon Town before moving to Wolves after a brief spell at Tottenham.

Only 22 when the war started, his way into the first team at Molineux had been barred by the legendary Stan Cullis.

But at Chelsea the centre-half spot was vacant and Harris, making his debut in August 1943, held the position down for the next 12 seasons before moving across to the right-back berth to accommodate Ron Greenwood.

Twice, in 1944 and 1945, he led his team-mates up the 39 steps at Wembley to receive wartime Cup Final medals, in Chelsea's first-ever appearances in the stadium. On the second occasion it was as a Cup winner, the trophy being presented by the Prime Minister, Mr Winston Churchill.

Harris dominated the defence with authority. A good organiser, he was an ideal tutor for young players coming into the side.

Two inches short of 6ft probably prevented more international recognition. Some also questioned his pace but in spite of both these supposed handicaps, his uncanny positional sense always took him into the right spot at the right time.

For almost 10 years he loyally soldiered on and must surely have cast longing glances to see lesser players picking up trophies and international honours.

But his second manager, Ted Drake, arriving at the Bridge in 1952 realised his value and although Drake bought his intended long-term replacement, Stan Wicks, Harris was on hand to slot into the right-back position when the regular occupant of that berth, Peter Sillett, was injured.

"I'll play anywhere you say, if you feel I can be of help to the side," he told his boss.

And a further 30 or so games in the number-two shirt not only prolonged his career beyond his 37th birthday, but most happily, also enabled him to win the League championship medal, seemingly out of reach for so long. The medal which he treasured above all others.

On the day the trophy was finally won, Saturday, 23 April 1955, John Harris was not playing but sitting anxiously in the directors' box.

But, of course, not unrecognised. As the team filed into the box, muddied and bedraggled at the end of certainly Chelsea's greatest day at that time, the fans demanded he came into the limelight in the front row.

A brief word or two was all that he could manage. Tears were not far away.

A year later he had gone, first to Chester as player-manager and then to the city of Sheffield, serving both United and Wednesday in turn for many years.

Chelsea Career

364 appearances   14 goals

Ron Harris – a record so safe

RECORDS, it is said, are made to be broken, but it is pretty safe to say that Ron Harris's total of 795 Chelsea first-team games is an achievement unlikely to be overtaken, or even approached, such are the ever-increasing demands of the modern game.

Harris was not blessed with outstanding talents – certainly so far as ball skills were concerned. But no one in Chelsea's history was more dedicated, more careful to maintain fitness, mental as well as physical.

Rarely, therefore, was his name not on the teamsheet once he had established an automatic right to his place.

No fewer than four times he was ever-present in a season's League games (42 in those days), and on seven occasions appeared in more than 50 Cup and League fixtures throughout a campaign.

Until the late autumn of his career, Harris knew no other club than Chelsea. Born in Hackney, he joined the juniors in August 1960 as a 15-year-old and signed professional forms 15 months later.

Already he had figured in Chelsea's FA Youth Cup-winning side and within three months he had made his first-team debut – manager Tommy Docherty ever-ready to give youth its head.

He was also brought into the side which clinched promotion from the Second Division in the spring of 1963 when Chelsea's challenge had begun to wobble. Thereby he proved himself for the big occasions.

His catalogue of club trophy successes is a lengthy one: after the FA Youth Cup, followed the Football League Cup (1965), the FA Cup (1970) and the European Cup-winners' Cup (1971) as well as two other Cup Final appearances.

What then were his particular talents? First, supreme fitness as a result of pursuing a punishing training programme. Dedication and self-discipline, Chelsea Football Club was simply his life.

Once, when asked what he would do if he won the football pools, he replied, "Make sure I was on time for training next morning."

As a captain, who skippered the side on more occasions than any other player before or since, he led by example, expecting others to match his own standards, a somewhat demanding target.

Of course, his methods frequently brought him into conflict with referees. 'Chopper' was never one to take prisoners.

Sadly, his final half-dozen seasons coincided with Chelsea's decline. Financial problems escalated and a string of players who had enjoyed the limelight of the club's golden years had either retired or moved on.

Not Ron Harris. He was impervious to disaster and misfortune and remained like a granite pinnacle protruding from a turbulent sea. Now he was tutoring the younger successors to those of Chelsea's victorious teams of a few year earlier.

The determination remained, even if the reactions and the legs responded less willingly.

Another sadness was the fact that Ron Harris never won honours for England above schoolboy and youth level. Maybe some though his style was too robust? His pace suspect? But many national teams of his generation could have benefited from his other qualities.

Chelsea Career

784-11 appearances   14 goals

Jack Harrow – never a bad game

IT has now become rare for a footballer to tie himself to one club throughout his entire career, let alone staying on to serve in a non-playing capacity for a further dozen years.

One such was Chelsea full-back Jack Harrow, who was signed from Croydon Common in March 1911.

His strength was, not least, his reliability. 'Never plays a bad game' was a tag frequently attached to his name.

Small for a full-back, standing just over 5ft 7in, he was speedy and especially quick into the tackle. And on the rare occasions when he was beaten to the ball, his pace enabled him to recover.

At junior level before, and Croydon Common, he first fulfilled his boyhood ambition to play at centre-forward.

Next stop was at wing-half (in which position he first attracted the attention of a Chelsea scout) before his manager experimented with him at full-back.

Chelsea paid £50 for his transfer to Stamford Bridge in March 1911 with a similar amount promised if he got into the first-team (a promise in fact never fulfilled).

For his first two seasons at Stamford Bridge he was a somewhat peripheral figure, usually plugging a gap at wing-half in emergency.

Then, in December 1913, five days before Christmas, he was selected at right-back and his long career was well and truly under way. Soon he was moved across to the other flank of the defence, where he remained until age inevitably took its toll, 13 years later, after he had suffered a facial injury which impaired his eyesight and judgement,

No Chelsea player of his time was more popular; no player more enthusiastic in his love of the game.

His total of 333 first-team games would, of course, have been considerably higher had he not lost four seasons during World War One.

While serving in the Royal Flying Corps he regularly escaped from his camp duties to make his way to Stamford Bridge, often playing under the pseudonym 'De Haviland'. None of the Chelsea regulars were fooled, of course, but it prevented, his Commanding Officer from discovering his absence from match reports in the press.

During the latter part of Harrow's career the new offside law was introduced which fundamentally changed the full-back's role.

Jack's views were outspoken. "The new law has killed full-back play," he said. "In my days there was a certain amount of art in the game. One back covered the other. Now the left-back covers one attacking flank and the right-back the other, with neither of them venturing up to the halfway line. The middle is closed up by the centre-half – or should be."

Since then of course, the game has again moved forward – not least so far as full-backs are concerned. This time Jack Harrow would undoubtedly have approved.

Harrow won two international caps for England and one for the Football League. And he was at his usual post for Chelsea in the 1914–15 FA Cup Final when he picked up a runners-up medal.

Until 1938 after Jack had finally hung up his boots he remained on the Stamford Bridge training staff, after which he retired to Mitcham where he lived up to the time of his death in July 1958.

Even to the end he retained interest in 'his club'. Visited by a Chelsea supporter in hospital he was clearly pleased to be remembered and to have the opportunity to relive the past.

Chelsea Career

333 appearances   5 goals

George Hilsdon – an instant success

VERY frequently down the years, from the very foundation of Chelsea Football Club to the present day, no expense has been spared to bring the biggest star attractions to Stamford Bridge. Not always, it must be confessed, with outstanding success.

Less frequent have been 'unknown' players whose potential had been spotted and such judgement quickly proved be justified.

One such was George Hilsdon, or 'Gatling Gun' as he was soon unofficially christened.

Near the end of Chelsea's first season, in the spring of 1906, manager Jackie Robertson travelled to Upton Park to spy on a West Ham United player who had been highly recommended.

"I never even set my eyes on the player I specially went to see. Instead they were glued all the time on the inside-left, a Cockney lad 19 years of age." Adding what turned out to be an accurate prophecy, Robertson said "If I get him he'll be our first-team centre-forward next season."

And so on 1 September 1906, George Hilsdon duly made his senior debut for Chelsea, against Glossop in the Second Division.

Even Jackie Robertson could not have anticipated such a startling and immediate dividend. The following day Hilsdon's name was emblazoned across every newspaper back page as he had scored five goals in Chelsea's 9-2 win.

Furthermore, he continued to live up to his newly-won reputation. Indeed, in an FA Cup-tie in January 1908 he went one better by scoring six times in another landslide victory, 9-1 against Worksop Town.

Nor did he confine himself to picking upon the lesser challenges of weaker opposition (107 goals from 164 first-team games being his final tally at Chelsea).

Within a month of joining Chelsea he was, not surprisingly, selected to play for the Football League against the Irish League in Belfast and scored a hat-trick in the visitors' 6-0 win.

Five full England caps were to follow; and they came at a time when competition to lead the attack was fierce and such fixtures limited almost entirely to home internationals, although he was a member of a short overseas tour in the summer of 1908, scoring twice in the opening game against Austria in Vienna and claiming another brace in England's final match.

Six goals in eight appearances for England was his final tally.

After three outstanding seasons in Chelsea's first team, including the club's first promotion to the First Division in the spring of 1907, George picked up a persistent injury in the early days of the 1909-10 season which undoubtedly was a factor in Chelsea's relegation.

Happily he regained his scoring touch the following campaign which was highlighted by the club's first appearance in an FA Cup semi-final, against Newcastle United, who won 3-0. Sadly, George sprained a tendon in training a few days before the game, a crucial blow for both club and player.

Never again did Hilsdon recapture his form or lethal shooting power. It was suggested that his ambition for a career in journalism was blunting his enthusiasm and commitment and he made his farewell appearance for Chelsea at Derby early in April 1912 before returning to wind down with his first love, West Ham United.

Ultimately retirement did not treat him kindly and he died at the age of 56, in Leicester in 1941.

He left behind a memory at Stamford Bridge, however. The mould for the weather vane which adorns the top of a stand represents George Hilsdon.

Chelsea Career

164 appearances   107 goals

Glenn Hoddle – bringer of intelligent football

BEYOND dispute, Glenn Hoddle was one of the most gifted footballers of his generation. For 12 seasons he was an integral part of Tottenham Hotspur's scene, making over 450 appearances and scoring more than a century of goals.

Not surprisingly, he was an automatic choice for England for almost a decade, winning 53 caps. And he appeared in four Cup Finals for Spurs.

When his playing career was nearing its end, it was obvious that he would continue in the game in a coaching or managerial capacity.

His brief stay at Swindon Town, fulfilling a dual role, was a useful experience en route to Stamford Bridge where he arrived, originally not to the universal satisfaction of supporters who felt that his predecessor, David Webb, was the man to steer Chelsea to a successful future.

But Ken Bates was firm in his choice, however, knowing what he planned: "I have always wanted Chelsea to play intelligent, exciting football and that has been lacking in recent years... in appointing Glenn Hoddle as manager I believe that we have taken the first step to getting Chelsea back to their traditional ways."

He had been at the Bridge before, spending six months as a Chelsea player in 1991 after leaving AS Monaco on a free transfer as he recovered from injury. Now aged 36, Glenn's days as a player were clearly nearing their end. But he managed to appear in almost half the games in his first season, if only rarely performing for the full 90 minutes.

At the heart of the action he could, of course, play and preach simultaneously, improving the technique of those around him. Both showing his superb passing skills and demonstrating 'how it should be done'.

Tactically he took it upon himself to introduce the sweeper system, with himself in the title role and as a *libero* rather than a mere extra defender. But the transition was never going to be easily achieved.

The somewhat unwieldy playing staff of 35 contained much dead wood and with some unable to adapt to new ideas. Disciplines could not be changed overnight.

But the quality of the play on view, with Chelsea emphasising the importance of keeping possession, improved markedly if not necessarily always reflected by results.

There was never a likelihood of mounting a serious challenge for Premiership honours. The League Cup campaign foundered at the second hurdle.

But the FA Cup brought success, as well as much needed income, as Hoddle's gospel began to reap dividends even if the opposition along the route to Wembley was not too demanding.

Perhaps the Final itself is best forgotten. Manchester United received some fortunate breaks after Chelsea had played most of the good football in the first half But, importantly, it was proof that Glenn Hoddle's leadership and ideas were bearing fruit. Everything had started to turn round.

And in his second season in charge, the improvement continued, even if the manager stepped on to the field as a player on ever more isolated occasions.

"Unfortunately in the end the legs go and my game has had to change," he said. And on the pitch he was confined to brief cameos.

Chelsea climbed three places up the Premiership and, if participation in both the Cup competitions was somewhat brief, some memorable European nights propelled the team into the semi-final of the Cup-winners' Cup, the tie agonisingly lost 4-3 on aggregate against Real Zaragoza.

But, conscious of limited finances and still lacking the necessary personnel to adapt to the 'Hoddle system', the manager was convinced he was 'getting there'.

Before this could be proved, however, he left Stamford Bridge to become manager of the England team, leaving the ideas he had implanted to be taken on by his successor, Ruud Gullitt. Alas, his career as England's manager was clouded by some controversial beliefs and, after taking his side to the 1998 World Cup finals, he left, later to reappear as manager of Southampton and then Spurs.

Chelsea Career

22-17 appearances   1 goals

John Hollins – never more faithfully

VERY few players down the years have served Chelsea longer, or more faithfully, than John Hollins. In addition to his two successful spells as a player at Stamford Bridge, he was also (less happily) manager of CFC from June 1985 to March 1988.

Born in Guildford, he arrived at Stamford Bridge in 1961 at the age of 15, but looking much younger, to join Chelsea's flourishing youth scheme.

So quickly did he become acclimatised to his new surroundings that his progression to professional status on the day he reached the age of 17 seemed natural – and automatic.

Two months later he made his first-team debut in a League Cup game at Swindon and a famous career was under way.

His enthusiasm was infectious; his energy never flagging, and it would be impossible to estimate the mileage he covered in nearly 600 games for Chelsea's cause.

A superb distributor of the ball, he constantly supplied his front-men with passes of pin-point accuracy, frequently joining in the fun himself with solo bursts followed by an often successful explosive strike on goal.

He was the complete midfield player. Well-timed tackles destroyed enemy attacks and transformed defence into attack in a flash with his vision to read the game.

He was never stationary, accompanying his game with high-pitched vocal cries of encouragement throughout the 90 minutes.

His Stamford Bridge career embraced 13 seasons in two instalments, but most surprisingly involved recognition by the England selectors on only one occasion, against Spain in 1967.

However, at club level, his sideboard was handsomely furnished by three major Cup-winners' medals and two Player-of-the-Year trophies as well as a clutch of more minor – but just as cherished – awards from supporters' clubs.

His days in SW6 came in two instalments. For 11 years he was part of the Chelsea team which matured into those highly successful seasons in which various trophies were won with narrow misses on several other occasions.

Consistency was not the least of his qualities. Rarely did his form dip; never did his commitment waver. In short, his contribution was simply taken for granted by his managers.

The parting of the ways, temporarily as it turned out, came with Chelsea's most successful-ever team up to that point being destroyed by internal dissent and temperamental outbursts as well as ill-discipline and refusal to conform to the manager's standards.

Successful spells at Queen's Park Rangers (four years) and Arsenal (for a similar period) almost closed his playing days.

But not before Stamford Bridge again beckoned and, at the age of 37, he returned to his *alma mater* playing another 36 first-team games (now moved into the back-four) and in reality joining John Neal as player-coach.

Twelve months later he was promoted to the managerial position for which he had been hand-picked by the chairman.

Thereafter, and sadly, it all went wrong. Discontent and rumour became rife. Morale plummeted and the team's performances deteriorated. After more than a dozen games without a single victory, John Hollins was sacked, walking away from Stamford Bridge among much bitterness and rancour.

An unhappy end for a wonderful Chelsea servant. Hurt and disillusioned, he had failed to communicate and instill into others those the very qualities which had been his trademark for over two decades.

Chelsea Career

592 appearances   64 goals

Peter Houseman – vibrant and successful

THE name Peter Houseman will always be linked with that era in the history of Chelsea Football Club when, after a difficult period of transition following the winning of the League championship title in 1954–55, manager Tommy Docherty was successfully building a new team largely based on talent emerging from the juniors.

Almost the whole of Peter's career at Stamford Bridge was as a member of a vibrant and successful period in the club's history.

His debut in December 1963 resulted in victory over Sheffield United. It was Chelsea's eighth game without defeat and, although he remained something of a fringe player for five seasons or so, ultimately he became an important part of a highly successful team.

'Nobby', as he was known, was basically an old-fashioned left-winger, but versatile enough to be called into service in midfield or, especially latterly in his Stamford Bridge career, at left-back.

As an attacker he possessed delicate footwork with an acceleration that would frequently leave defenders trailing in his wake. Probably his most telling asset of all, though, was the ability to pin-point his crosses on to the heads of such as Peter Osgood, Ian Hutchinson and Tommy Baldwin.

Thus, a relatively modest output of 31 goals from some nearly 350 games is an entirely misleading statistic.

Be that as it may, one goal will always stand in the memory. As half-time approached in the 1970 FA Cup Final against Leeds United at Wembley, Chelsea, thoroughly out of sorts, were trailing 1-0, whereupon Peter's shot somehow eluded Gary Sprake's dive entirely to alter the run of play – and destroy the previous confidence of the opposition.

Two months earlier, two of his occasional goals had salvaged an apparently lost cause in a fourth-round FA Cup replay at Burnley and, still not content, Peter laid on a typically measured centre for Tommy Baldwin to put Chelsea into the lead and on course for Wembley.

At the age of 30, he was transferred to Oxford United in May 1975 for a £30,000 fee.

Probably it was a wise move for Houseman; Chelsea's most successful side up to that time was disintegrating and the dressing-room was seemingly unsettled and divisive.

Used both as a winger and also in midfield, operating behind the strikers, he was an automatic first-team choice for his 22 months at the Manor Ground.

One local reporter commented that his crosses from the flanks and general use of the ball are 'of an accuracy rarely seen at The Manor before'.

And then Peter, along with his wife and two friends, were killed in a car crash in March 1977, leaving six children without parents.

Two testimonial matches took place, at Stamford Bridge and at Oxford, and 31 teammates and colleagues from Chelsea attended Peter Houseman's funeral service. Such was the high regard in which he was held.

Chelsea Career

325-18 appearances   39 goals

Alan Hudson – just brilliant

IN an age when established stars from many parts of the world are converging on the English Premiership, it is pertinent to recall that one Chelsea star of some 30 years ago was born and bred within easy walking distance of Stamford Bridge.

Alan Hudson's early education into the game came via his father, Bill, who well prepared him for the only career that was remotely likely for the lad.

Arriving as an apprentice and enormously gifted and tactically wise beyond his years, he made the transition into the senior team, via a brief acquaintance with Combination football. His League debut came at Southampton on 1 February 1969, before he went back to the Reserves until the start of the following season.

And that 1969–70 season remains, of course, one of the most famous in the club's history.

"He is not in the side on sentiment," manager Dave Sexton informed the media. "He is a fine young player and the way he organises things in midfield is first-class."

'Huddy' would direct play with a waving of his arms and his distribution of the ball, both in inch-perfect accuracy and range, was just brilliant.

Moving forward from deep positions, he ran at defences before splitting them apart with his precise well-timed through passes.

For six months in that season he was rarely out of the headlines, with even Sir Alf Ramsay, not normally one given to extravagant praise, acknowledging the boy's capabilities and genius.

By Easter 1970, Chelsea had already reserved their place in the FA Cup Final and were occupying fourth spot in the First Division table.

Then, at West Bromwich, Hudson tore his ankle ligaments and was forced to miss the Cup Final and, indeed, the rest of that season.

Happily he was back again for the beginning of the 1970–71 campaign and was once more an integral part of the team which went on to win the European Cup-winners' Cup in Athens.

But, with hindsight, it is fair to say that thereafter in his last three seasons at the Bridge he never quite scaled those earlier heights, or achieved the previous high consistency.

Memories remain. There was his extraordinary strike in a Football League Cup semi-final second leg at Tottenham when he scored the deciding goal seconds before the final whistle, by steering a free-kick from a difficult angle through a forest of legs as the Spurs goalkeeper Pat Jennings and his defenders hesitated and dithered.

Yet perhaps, the most remarkable of all was at Coventry on the last day of February 1970.

Picking up a pass on the edge of his own penalty area, Alan, shaking off a series of tackles, ran fully 70 yards before calmly steering the ball past the 'keeper and into the net.

Yet, unhappily, along with others, Alan's relationship with manager Dave Sexton soured. Hudson was dropped from the side on New Year's Day 1974 and never played in Chelsea's first-team again, despite returning to the Bridge briefly nine years later, when illness and injury sidelined him.

Two international caps, both won after he left the Bridge, make a mockery of what he had to offer at the highest level.

Thereafter his career continued at Stoke City (1974–76), where he gained further international recognition, and Arsenal (1976–78), followed by stays with Seattle Sounders and Stoke City (again) before that brief and somewhat fruitless return to Chelsea.

Chelsea Career

118-1 appearances   14 goals

Mark Hughes – always a winner

THE arrival of Mark Hughes at Stamford Bridge, at the age of 33, was a surprise to most people.

Old Trafford had always been his spiritual home, although he had sampled European club football both with Barcelona and Bayern Munich (on loan). Even so, Manchester United had been regarded as 'his club'.

He was a product of their junior system, beginning as a midfield player before being converted to the centre-forward role in which he became famous.

His debut in senior first-team football was in October 1983 and five months later he became a regular in United's League side.

His collection of medals would fill the largest of cabinets (two Premiership championships, three FA Cups, and a League Cup winner, two FA Charity Shield winners' medals (and one shared) as well as a European Cup winners' and a European Super Cup winners' medal. Along his 12-year route in the North-West he represented Wales on 65 occasions, as well as winning two PFA Player of the Year awards.

If Chelsea fans could never argue against such a pedigree, there were reservations among some about how much petrol remained in the tank. However, any such concerns were soon to be dismissed.

He opened his goalscoring account on his fourth appearance at the Bridge with a stunning drive against Coventry City. His output, impressive enough, would have been even greater had he not been forced to miss nine games through suspensions.

His physical strength was a formidable asset and his sphere of operation involved the entire area between both penalty boxes.

He was a superb target man, holding up play, dismissing all challenges to take the ball away, before wheeling round and liberating a more advantageously placed colleague. It was, of course, his massive physique which made it virtually impossible to dispossess him.

During his first Chelsea season he spent most of his time as a lone striker with two inside-forwards playing off him. Then, he benefited from the arrival of Gianfranco Zola, with whom he established a happy liaison. Two men of totally contrasting styles, and of different build, but each with fertile footballing brains.

Probably the game for which he is best remembered is the unforgettable fourth-round FA Cup-tie against Liverpool at Stamford Bridge in January 1997.

'Sparky' was omitted from the starting line-up (he had missed two days training the previous week) and, at half-time, Chelsea found themselves two goals behind after two bad defensive errors.

With Chelsea changing to an unusual 3-3-1-3 formation, Hughes was already awaiting the reappearance of the referee on the touchline, pawing the turf like a raging bull anxious to enter the arena (to replace Scott Minto) after the half-time break.

Within five minutes he had rifled in an unstoppable shot to reduce the arrears and, with his aggression and tireless running, went on to inspire a famous 4-2 victory

As one reporter put it, 'He was a constantly exploding bomb from the second he came on. His 45 minutes was the performance of the season.'

He never regretted his move to Chelsea. "I knew which direction the club was going and what the club were trying to achieve and that was the attraction of coming."

His playing career, finally winding down at Blackburn, came to its inevitable close by which time he had been appointed manager of Wales with whom his impact has been just as positive on the touchline as it was as a player.

Mark Hughes is, and always has been, a winner.

Chelsea Career

109-14 appearances   39 goals

Ian Hutchinson – fairytale beginning, tragic end

THERE have been few more popular players at Stamford Bridge down the years than Ian Hutchinson. Equally, there have also been few, if any, who have been more unlucky.

His career had a fairytale beginning. First spotted by Nottingham Forest while playing for a local works side, he was taken on as junior for 18 months or so before being rejected, whereupon he joined Burton Albion, then in the old Southern League and where one of his colleagues in the forward line was Richie Barker, who later enjoyed good days under Brian Clough at Derby, before himself becoming a manager.

Cambridge United, then also in the Southern League, was Hutchinson's next stopping place whereupon fate took a hand.

It was to the university town that Frank Blunstone was despatched to run his eye over the local goalkeeper. Instead he returned with a glowing report about the United's tall, well-built and powerful centre-forward.

Visits from Chelsea manager Dave Sexton and assistant manager Ron Suart swiftly followed and so 'Hutch' was hurriedly brought to Stamford Bridge, interrupting his honeymoon to sign on the dotted line.

Within three months he had made his first-team debut at Derby (a couple of miles or so from where he was born), and straight away struck up an easy understanding, and formidable partnership, with Peter Osgood. Indeed, in their first full season (1969–70) together they scored more than 50 goals.

That year Chelsea won the FA Cup for the first time in their history as the club looked ahead with greater confidence and optimism than ever before.

Yet, sadly, that was to prove the peak of Ian Hutchinson's career. All too soon, problems with a knee caused a prolonged absence from the team and were ultimately to end his career. A twice-broken leg merely added to his misfortunes.

No patient could have been braver. Refusing to accept medical opinion, he made various, and brave, comebacks when lesser men would have bowed to the inevitable.

"After each operation I had to learn to walk again," he said after his career had finally ended. "Then how to run to catch a bus and so on. People suggested that my style of play was the cause of my injury problems. But I honestly don't think so."

That style was flamboyant and there were natural gifts in abundance. He was fast, with further acceleration kept in reserve. For a heavily-built man, his ball control was excellent, and, making full use of his height, he had excellent heading ability.

Sometimes his teammates had doubts about his tactical play, for he was both innovative and unpredictable. But this was much more problematic to opponents than to colleagues.

And then, of course, his long throw-in, which exceeded even that of Sam Weaver 40 years before. Better than a corner was a frequent verdict and it was from one of these prodigious throws that David Webb headed the winning goal to bring the FA Cup to Stamford Bridge for the first time, 18 days after Hutchinson had made the replay possible by scoring an equalising goal in the dying minutes of the first game at Wembley.

"The goal I will always remember," he often said later.

Fate had dealt him a rough hand as a player; increasingly his last days before his death in 2002 were tragic – and almost as painful for his host of friends and admirers as to Ian himself.

Chelsea Career

137-7 appearances   58 goals

Erland Johnsen – supreme in defence

THE careers of some players run smoothly; others, for a variety of reasons, run into problems. One such was Erland Johnsen, who was born in Frederikstad and had already won 14 international caps for Norway when he arrived at Stamford Bridge, from Bayern Munich, in December 1989 for a £306,000 fee.

Immediately winning his place in the League side, and partnering Ken Monkou in central defence, injury and loss of form caused him to play only a handful of games during his second and third seasons at Chelsea, by which time Paul Elliott had arrived on the scene to increase the challenge for first-team football (and Erland was unsettled when informed by the Norwegian international management that he needed to play at the highest level if he wished to resurrect his international career).

However, David Webb, in his short spell in the managerial post, was quick to spot Erland's strength (in what, of course, had been Webb's own position) and the arrival of Glenn Hoddle as manager gave him a new opportunity finally to establish himself as first-choice centre-half in the 1993–94 season which he crowned with an FA Cup Final appearance, as well as a return, after four years, to the Norwegian international side, playing both at Wembley and in the World Cup.

Even better times, so far as his Chelsea career was concerned, arrived when, with Hoddle certainly bringing out the best in him, he was voted Player of the Year in 1995.

Even then, however, competition was keen for defensive positions and Michael Duberry edged him out of the team in the winter of 1996, occasionally with Erland finding himself operating on the left flank of the defence which was never his forte.

Some games, especially, stick out in the memory. Many felt that he was the catalyst in the well-remembered comeback in the European Cup-winners' Cup quarter-final against Bruges in March 1995 when, with others claiming the banner headlines, Erland was described by one critic as 'supreme in defence' and the player famously said, "In that great atmosphere when we went out of the tunnel we just knew that we were going to beat them."

Another oft-recalled occasion was an epic FA Cup-tie against Leicester City in a fifth-round replay at Stamford Bridge in February 1997.

Extra-time was almost exhausted. Chelsea had hit the woodwork twice but neither side had managed to score when the Norwegian, who had come on as a substitute 15 minutes earlier, bulldozed his way out of defence, and moving forward at high speed, played a 'one-two' with Vialli and, amidst a flurry of arms and legs, collapsed to the ground. Instantly referee Mike Reed awarded a penalty. Leicester protested furiously – and with much justification – before Frank Leboeuf rattled the ball into the net and settled the tie.

An hour later in a nearby restaurant, and surrounded by happy Chelsea fans, Erland reacted to all enquiries about the incident silently, but with a wink and a mischievous grin.

Out of contract, the Norwegian sensibly felt that the uncertainty of his place in the Chelsea's Premiership side could have affected his ambitions for the national side and decided it was time to return home.

In his final game he was captain for the day and received a wonderful ovation from a 27,000 crowd. Subsequently, at the FA Cup Final dinner, he was presented by the chairman with an engraved glass bowl, to acknowledge his loyal and faithful service.

Bayern Munich or Chelsea? "On the day the German team was not better than the Chelsea side I left behind." Although Stamford Bridge was not as formidable as the Bayern fortress, Erland noticed a marked change of attitude in visiting teams during his days at the Bridge. Respect and more of a sense of fear.

Chelsea Career

170-13 appearances   1 goals

Tommy Law – an unlikely legend

IT is interesting, albeit perhaps somewhat pointless, to speculate how Tommy Law would have fared in modern football. Somewhat portly and certainly lacking in pace, not only was he a fixture at left-back for Chelsea for almost 10 seasons, he was also a member of Scotland's 'Wembley Wizards' who so humiliated England in 1928.

And, seeing him stumping along the gloomy corridor behind the old East Stand at Stamford Bridge and up into his seat in the 1950s and 1960s, long after his playing days were over, no-one would never have identified him as a professional footballer, let alone one of the game's legends.

The basis of his success was his wonderful football brain which instilled in him an uncanny positional sense. He was very quick of thought, demonstrating the extent to which a footballer's head can save his legs.

Spotted by Chelsea's Scottish scout when Law was playing for the Glasgow club, Waverley, he arrived in London (where he was to spend the rest of his life – he died in February 1976 aged 68) in June 1925, for the statutory signing-on fee of £10, having played in only five competitive games for his junior club.

Settling in London, and at Stamford Bridge, was no problem. For when Tommy made his First Division debut on 18 September 1926, he was one of seven Scotsmen in the team.

And from the day of that first appearance he remained an automatic choice at left-back for the next seven seasons.

His secret, of course, was his reading of a game. Law was always on hand to clear up danger. He would break up opposing attacks with clever interceptions (often incurring the wrath of opposition fans who mistakenly blamed their own player for inaccurate passing) and then quickly launch a Chelsea attack with a first-time ball.

Such was his skill and accuracy that he could pick out a colleague in an open space, even 50 yards away.

Rarely caught in possession, he was missing from his post only rarely in his first four seasons at Stamford Bridge. And in two of those campaigns Chelsea had fewer goals scored against than any team in their division.

In fact he was a major contributor to Chelsea's return to the First Division in May 1930, after six seasons out of the top flight, the club's longest spell outside the League championship race.

A modest man, Tommy would reminisce about that Scottish 5-1 victory at Wembley. "My only regret that my fellow Scot and Chelsea partner, George Smith wasn't there as well. He was a better back than I was."

Some would not agree, but it was typical of Tommy's modesty.

A conscientious player, he never played for any other club after Chelsea. He refused an offer to move to France to play for Nimes, which would have doubled his wages and where he would have joined his Chelsea colleague, Alex Cheyne.

The Nimes club knew his worth. And fortunately so did Chelsea.

Chelsea Career

319 appearances   19 goals

Tommy Lawton – Chelsea were privileged

LOOKING back, it was a privilege for Chelsea Football Club to have had the services of Tommy Lawton, one of the greatest centre-forwards in England's history, albeit for only exactly two years – and that included six months of wartime regional football.

Born in Bolton, Lawton became the most expensive 17-year-old in the game when he moved from Burnley to Everton for £6,500, in 1936.

A little over two years later he had won a Football League championship medal with the Merseysiders (34 goals in 38 games) and established his place as England's centre-forward, scoring the winning goal against Scotland at Hampden Park before a crowd of 130,000.

Then, like so many of his generation, his League career was suspended for seven years while he served in the Army as a CSM during World War Two, although he did play in 15 unofficial international games for his country.

Coming to London and signing for Chelsea was a sensation. More than 50,000 flocked into Stamford Bridge to witness his debut in a regional league game against Birmingham City. Three days later the audience had doubled as surely Chelsea's biggest-ever home attendance came to watch the Londoners – Lawton and all – take on the might of Russia's Moscow Dynamo, a mystery team who had created an air of fascination. The official figure was 74,496 but it is estimated that about 100,000 were present, beating the 82,905 who saw Arsenal in October 1935.

"When I arrived at Stamford Bridge that Tuesday afternoon it seemed that everyone in London had taken the day off. The crush was so great that the police had to clear a path for us to get on the field. The Russians were brilliant but even so, with eight minutes remaining I nodded Chelsea into a 3-2 lead.

"We thought we'd won but then one of their forwards beat Vic Woodley, our goalkeeper, after receiving the ball 25 yards offside!"

Quietly the referee whispered to Tommy, "I had to give it for diplomatic reasons!"

They were unsettling days at Stamford Bridge. Manager Billy Birrell was desperately trying to construct a new team, his pre-war side of seven years earlier having vanished into retirement.

In the summer of 1947, Chelsea ordered Lawton to go on a tour of Sweden, but the player, not unreasonably, protested; he had gone 18 months without a break and, returning from an England match in Portugal, had picked up a touch of food poisoning. Unknown to him, his presence on the tour had been written into the contract. However, he stuck to his guns and remained behind.

Relations with the board and manager soured from then on, even though Lawton later in admitted some of the disputes were of his own making: "I felt I was too big to take unreasonable orders."

So the marriage between club and player broke up. Both Arsenal and Sunderland were interested in obtaining his services but, almost unbelievably, it was Third Division South club Notts County who were successful (their manager was a good friend of Tommy's) and he went on to become the first player from that division to play for England.

But it is interesting to speculate how his latter footballing days would have shaped if he had remained in the top flight of his profession.

Later his life was clouded by a series of personal problems but towards the end the light began to shine for him again when the *Nottingham Evening Post* gave him a regular weekly column and he appeared at Notts County's social club for a '*This is Your Life*' evening, attended by almost all his former colleagues of 30 years before.

His column became a feature in the city, his respect restored. And he found himself again fêted and recognised for what he had been. One of football's greats. Tommy Lawton died in Nottingham in November 1996, aged, 77.

Chelsea Career

53 appearances   35 goals

Frank Leboeuf – he had them spellbound

WITHIN minutes of Frank Leboeuf making his League debut for Chelsea, against Southampton at The Dell, old-timers who had made the journey down from London to welcome the new season were spellbound. Not since Peter O'Dowd had they seen a centre-half with such superb technique.

Leboeuf's expert and almost casual – at times perhaps too casual – tidying up of threatening situations at the back immediately caught the eye. He saw his role as that of a *libero*, and constantly came forward, never feeling himself obliged to be chained deep inside his defence.

He was alert and reacted to situations, invariably carrying him into the right place at the right time, and always doing so apparently unhurriedly, suggesting it was merely the simple, and obvious, thing to do.

Yet he realised he had much to learn from the English game and, in this, he was greatly helped by Chelsea's new manager, Ruud Gullit.

Rather than accepting what he found, Gullit transformed things that had long been the accepted practice in League football in England.

No defender used the ball out of defence more quickly, more accurately, or more intelligently, than Leboeuf and this was made seemingly simpler because he was naturally two-footed.

But what made him stand out above others of his position in England was the range of his accurate passing from the back. So gifted was he in this particular art that it seemed as if he was almost stroking the ball to the foot of any colleague up to 50 yards distant, as if guided by a magnet. Who could forget his chipped pass to set up Zola's winning goal in the European Cup-winners' Cup Final in Stockholm?

Yet he did not immediately find the transition into the Football League easy, despite the impression he gave. "For me it was more difficult because I had to work hard physically and run a lot." But soon he had conquered most problems, off as well as on the field, and his family settled most happily in London.

And, of course, such accuracy was also an asset when his surges upfield brought him within range of the opposing goal. He would unleash a shot of tremendous power and accuracy, the ball often skidding through close to the surface of the ground.

Nine of his goals came in this way (alongside 15 penalties). Probably the best remembered was his brilliant equaliser in the UEFA quarter-final against AC in Milan.

Inevitably perhaps, he had his shortcomings.

On occasions a hefty charge from an opponent would see him collapse as if agony and seemingly out for the count, writhing theatrically, as colleagues gathered round. Seconds later he would be up on his feet and apparently none the worse for wear.

At other times he would rise to the bait when verbally abused by the opposition and his responses would sometimes result in disciplinary action against him.

But any such failings were well outweighed by his abundant gifts, that technical flair, and his reading of a game; his deceptive pace and positive well-timed tackling.

Certainly he would be a serious candidate for any all-time Chelsea XI.

During his time in this country he won 32 international caps and was in France's 1998 World Cup Final team against Brazil.

Unfortunately he was a contemporary of France's captain, Laurent Blanc, who kept him out of the national team at times. And on one occasion a sending-off did him no favours with the selectors.

It was for his native country that he left Chelsea in the summer of 2001 signing for Marseille at a fee of £1.2 million.

He was one of Chelsea's greatest-ever stars. Few down the years have possessed such a wide range of gifted skills.

Chelsea Career

200-4 appearances   15 goals

Graeme Le Saux – an outstanding player and personality

DURING his time at Stamford Bridge, Graeme Le Saux has become one of Chelsea's outstanding players, as well as being a leading personality.

He was signed from Jersey at the age of 19, in December 1987, on a free transfer, and made his debut in the first team some 18 months later, as a substitute.

From the start he took the eye and became a firm favourite with the fans through his dedication and enthusiasm.

That he was always going to be a spectacular player was clear from his first full appearance, on Boxing Day 1989, when he scored a last-minute equaliser in a 2-2 draw against Crystal Palace at Selhurst Park. This after he had been booked – and not by any means for the last time in his career.

His game is essentially based on total commitment. Losing the ball merely presents a challenge to win it back, in the quickest time possible,

One of his particular hallmarks, of course, is his explosive pace which sees him surging down the open spaces on the left wing before crossing the ball, agonisingly out of the goalkeeper's reach to the far post, to the consternation of opponents, and to excitement of his fans.

It was strange that his Chelsea career was interrupted by a four-year period, from March 1993 to August 1997, when he signed for Blackburn Rovers for a fee of £625,000. As Chelsea director, Colin Hutchinson later admitted, "Selling him was a mistake which took £5 million pounds to rectify."

But not a mistake for Graeme Le Saux, who won a Premiership championship medal at Ewood Park in 1995.

Previously he had not been the most popular member of the dressing-room. However, on his return it was a 'different' Chelsea into which he fitted more easily and became instantly accepted, for a few years representing the club on the PFA as well as being the first-team vice-captain. Absence had indeed made the heart grow fonder.

One of the unexplained factors in Le Saux's career has been his regular absence from the England team. Admittedly he has won 36 full caps for his country, and played in the 1998 World Cup finals in France.

But at a time when the various national managers have been searching for left-footed players, in defence, midfield and attack, it is strange that he did not again find favour, And, not least, because his versatility allows him to be equally proficient at full-back or on the left side of midfield in a 4–3–3.

However his career has by no means been without its rewards.

Apart from his championship medal with Blackburn, he was a squad member of Chelsea's European Cup-winners' Cup team, while four months later he was playing in the side against Real Madrid which won the European Super Cup.

And his trophy cabinet also includes a League Cup winners' medal and a similar memento from the 1998 FA Charity Shield.

And still no one is more hungry to add to this already impressive collection.

Chelsea Career

280-32 appearances   39 goals

Jim Lewis – an amateur first and foremost

JAMES Leonard Lewis was an amateur footballer first and foremost. The son of James William, himself a distinguished international for both Great Britain and England, his first appearance in the professional game was on Boxing Day 1950 when he turned out for Leyton Orient against Watford in the Third Division South.

But, like his father, Walthamstow Avenue was his club and it was made abundantly clear to Orient that they retained first call on his services.

As a result, he played only three more games for them, all in that 1950–51 season, two at centre-forward and one on the right wing, without managing to get his name on the scoresheet.

Almost two years later, and already having represented England at amateur level himself, he was again lured away from Isthmian League football, this time by Chelsea manager, Ted Drake, less than two months into his first season at Stamford Bridge. Jim made his First Division debut against Charlton Athletic at The Valley, when, faced with rebuilding the side Chelsea, in mid-table, were trailing Charlton 2-1 at half-time – the home team having been awarded two penalty-kicks (scoring from only one of them).

Lewis, who had started the game on the right wing, was then moved into the middle, allowing Bobby Campbell to return to his normal position. Certainly the move paid a rich dividend when he obtained the equaliser in a 2-2 draw, with a header.

"The switch was a ready-made one," said Drake afterwards, "pre-arranged if things were not going well. We hope to see more of Jim in Chelsea colours."

He was mindful that Lewis' strong allegiance with Walthamstow would limit his involvement at Stamford Bridge, although he did turn out in almost half of Chelsea's games the following season.

Not the least of Lewis's value was the fact that he could operate equally happily on either wing, or at centre-forward.

In the 1954–55 Football League championship season he was able to deputise for wingers Parsons and Blunstone, as well as Roy Bentley, in the centre-forward position.

And when Blunstone was injured, in the first match of the season, Lewis took over at outside-left until Blunstone returned at the beginning of November.

The two men could not have presented a greater contrast. Lewis, almost five inches taller than Blunstone, used his turn of speed as well as clever footwork, to take him past defenders, his long legs skipping over tackles, and he would create scoring opportunities both for himself and the central attackers.

He was also a fine header of the ball, along with Roy Bentley and Les Stubbs forming a threatening trio, especially at corner kicks.

The championship won, he remained at Stamford Bridge for a further three seasons, filling in on either wings whenever, for reasons of injury, either Parsons or Blunstone were absent.

His happy association, spread over six seasons, ended in April 1958 when he was presented with an illuminated address to commemorate his distinguished career at Stamford Bridge.

Indeed, it had been a most fruitful association.

Chelsea Career

95 appearances   40 goals

Gary Locke – a light in days of darkness

THROUGH no fault of his own Gary Locke's name is seldom in the forefront of discussions about Chelsea's past.

A product of the club's youth scheme, he made his debut in a Second Division fixture at Coventry on the last day of September 1972, taking over the right-back position from Ron Harris whose presence had been more urgently required in central defence.

The following week the Chelsea programme acknowledged Locke's debut as 'impressive'.

At the age of 18, he had already won an England Youth international cap and Paddy Mulligan, also another recent holder of the number-two shirt, had been sold to Crystal Palace.

Sexton's confidence in the youngster was immediately justified and he had established himself as an automatic choice until dislocating his shoulder, whilst keeping goal in a six-a-side training session. His absence, though, proved only brief.

At the end of that season Chelsea finished in 12th spot and, despite the presence of such as Harris, David Webb, Peter Osgood and (briefly) Charlie Cooke, there were few positives to be drawn, with five consecutive defeats in March and April merely an early sign of troubles ahead.

Locke's qualities as a defender were based on sound foundations. He was ever solid and reliable. His tackles were firm and well-timed. He was adept in shepherding an opponent from dangerous situations in the penalty area away to the corner flag. Especially remembered are his skill in blocking crosses from the flanks.

He possessed good pace and acceleration, and few players in direct opposition could ever claim to have emerged on top of the contest.

Nor was he a purely defensive full-back. Obtaining possession in his own area, he would bring the ball out of danger through a gap before accelerating, legs working like pistons, and arriving at the other end of the field to get in a dangerous centres on to the heads of the central attackers.

Then the operation completed, he would sprint back to his own quarter of the field to the warm cheers of his fans.

Unfortunately, his 11 seasons in the first team were periodically interrupted by injuries. In only seven of these campaigns as an automatic choice for the right-back berth did appear in as many as half of the fixtures.

So a total of over 300 senior appearances could have been substantially greater had good fortune come his way.

Equally, if his career had coincided with Chelsea's days of richer achievement, Gary would certainly have been a valuable recruit.

He was approaching his 30th birthday, and then in a side whose ambitions were focussed in avoiding relegation to Division Three, when his Stamford Bridge career was ended with the arrival of Joey Jones. Whereupon Gary crossed the river to Selhurst Park, playing exactly 100 first-team games for Crystal Palace before finally ending his career in Sweden.

Definitely a Chelsea legend whose light shone so many through days of darkness.

Chelsea Career

315-2 appearances   4 goals

Eddie McCreadie – gamble that paid a rich dividend

IN April 1962, Chelsea Football Club was at its lowest ebb for more than 30 years. The previous season, a sequence of 11 games which had yielded only four points, all from drawn games, had left the club marooned at the bottom of the First Division table.

Months before, Ted Drake, architect of the 1954–55 championship team, had departed, leaving an inexperienced side floundering helplessly with Tommy Docherty, under the title of chief coach, left to cut his teeth on a task of re-structuring the professional staff.

Fortunately, he had a good reservoir of talented young players, but a dearth of experience, to offer the required guidance and example.

Into this somewhat unpromising situation strode a 22-year-old, raw-boned Scotsman, also short of playing experience at a high level, Eddie McCreadie.

The £5,000 fee paid to East Stirling for his services appeared something of a gamble. But almost straight away it became obvious it would pay a rich dividend.

He was a strong left-footed full-back in the modern style, ever ready to steam forward out of defence and participate in raids down the flank.

Partnering Ken Shellito, on the other side of the defence, the two became the best full-back pairing in the Second Division. And Docherty had unearthed a player he described as "a gem buried in the lower division of the Scottish League".

At once Chelsea discarded the despairing misfortunes of the previous season and soared to the top of the League before – after a worrying spell in the New Year aggravated by a long break in the League programme due to the severe winter – they won promotion the following May.

McCreadie may not have been the most cultured or most skilful of full-backs. And he could be impetuous, committing himself rashly, or mistiming a tackle.

But, more usually, he would shackle his opposing winger, yet still find time to rescue other colleagues – frequently employing an 'elastic' left foot to slide the ball away to safety, often when a goal had seemed inevitable – or surge forward into the attack.

No cause was ever lost when Eddie McCreadie was marauding at the heart of Chelsea's defence.

Sometimes he would insist on playing when a lesser man would have been sidelined by injury. Occasionally he would be employed as an emergency centre-forward.

And no one present will forget his goal, against Leicester City, ten minutes from time in the first-leg of the Football League Cup Final at Stamford Bridge in March 1965.

With Chelsea reduced to 10 men, Eddie embarked on an 80-yard dash, by-passing a series of opponents as if they did not exist, before firing the ball into the net past a startled Gordon Banks, and then sinking to his knees in sheer exhaustion.

As the Chelsea *Official Programme* editor put it, 'The goal belongs among the finest solo efforts in 60 years of football at Stamford Bridge.'

Having retired as a player, McCreadie managed the Combination side and then succeeded Dave Sexton as coach to the senior squad.

Operating under severe financial restrictions, he produced virtually a new team which achieved promotion against the odds in the spring of 1977, only for him to fall out with the chairman regarding a dispute over a new contract.

Consequently, Chelsea, and British football, were the losers as Eddie McCreadie disappeared to work in North American soccer.

Chelsea Career

405-5 appearances   5 goals

John McNichol – purveyor of the Bovril Ball

THERE is, not surprisingly, an aura surrounding Chelsea's 1954–55 Football League championship team. And an integral part of that team was John McNichol.

A Scotsman, born in Kilmarnock, McNichol played no senior football north of the border. Newcastle United was his first professional club, but surprisingly, while on Tyneside for two seasons, he never made an appearance in the Football League either.

It was with Brighton and Hove Albion that he first made his mark, and it was in the South Coast town that he settled down and made his permanent home.

When manager Ted Drake arrived at Stamford Bridge in May 1952, having learnt his trade at Reading, he brought with him an intimate working knowledge of players in the lower divisions, of the Football League and his first signing on taking up office at Chelsea was John McNichol, then aged 27.

It may seem a relatively late time in a playing career to step up two divisions into the country's most cut-throat league. But John made the transition easily and with a minimum of fuss.

His Scottish background was betrayed by his mastery of ball skills. Everything he did on the football pitch revealed a football brain. He was a schemer who could unlock opposing defences with shrewd distribution.

But unlike many of the type, he was also a regular goalscorer, averaging one for every three games played for Chelsea.

Ted Drake's second signing for Chelsea was Ron Greenwood, later of course to become a most successful manager, and Greenwood was one of McNichol's greatest admirers.

He would recall how John had the rare ability to curve shots and passes with the outside of his foot and was a player who 'made things happen'.

One such was humorously known as the 'Bovril Ball', a long pass which McNichol would direct towards the prominent Bovril advertisement on a corner at the north end of the Bridge. This was designed – and perfectly weighted – for his right winger, little Eric Parsons, to run on to and it became a fertile source of crosses leading to goals at that end of the ground.

As both provider and finisher, McNichol was the complete inside-forward and it was something of a mystery that he lay largely undiscovered until the middle years of his career.

Winning the Football League championship was, of course, the pinnacle in his football life and he always looked back with nostalgia on that 1954–55 season.

The 6-5 defeat in the home fixture against Manchester United left Chelsea dawdling below halfway in the table, and two further defeats suggested none of the excitement which was to come.

Then followed the remarkable renaissance in the ensuing 24 fixtures, which produced 14 victories and six draws.

"Those days will always stand out in my memory – and I will never forget my first FA Cup-tie. I cracked two ribs in the first game at Derby but didn't know about it until the replay!"

But it is that championship season that lingers longest in the memory. Operating alongside centre-forward Roy Bentley and with outside-right Parsons, together they provided almost 50 goals in that famous season.

Chelsea Career

202 appearances   66 goals

Harry Medhurst – entitled to his place in history

THE name of Harry Medhurst tends not to enter into discussions about the long and distinguished list of Chelsea's goalkeepers. Yet he is certainly entitled to a place in the club's history.

Like many of his generation, his career was decimated by World War Two. Born in Woking, he was signed by West Ham United in 1936, at the age of 20, and made his Football League debut for the Hammers against Fulham at Upton Park on Christmas Eve two years later, holding his place in the first team for the rest of that last pre-war season.

During the war, and stationed in the Home Counties, he played whenever available and was an ever-present in West Ham's transitional season of 1945–46.

However, the arrival of a local lad, Ernie Gregory, ended Medhurst's spell as first-choice 'keeper and, now past 30, he moved across London to Stamford Bridge in December 1946, to succeed the legendary Vic Woodley, a transfer which involved Chelsea's Joe Payne travelling in the other direction in part-exchange.

Immediately Medhurst became a popular figure at the Bridge. Only 5ft 8in in height, he made up for his lack of inches with his agility, allied to good anticipation and complete fearlessness.

At school Harry had taken no interest in football but later enlisted for a local team and played at outside-left before filling a gap as an emergency 'keeper, thereby following in the steps of his father who was a well-known amateur player.

This led to his move up the ladder to sign for Woking FC, for whom he kept goal for three seasons prior to joining West Ham.

A fruit farmer and landscape gardener by profession, he was an all-round athlete, having played Minor Counties cricket for Cambridgeshire and lawn tennis in various local competitions.

With his ready smile, he at once won over Chelsea fans. During his five seasons in the League team he was operating behind a somewhat ageing and ponderous defence which at least managed to maintain the club's place in the top division, albeit often with a little to spare.

Two games stand out in Harry's time at Chelsea. In January 1948, against Derby County at the Baseball Ground on a quagmire of a pitch, the Rams, marshalled by Raich Carter and Billy Steel and with the massive Jack Stamps at centre-forward, simply ran riot. With all three figuring on the scoresheet, the Rams won 5-1.

What the score does not indicate was the fact that Harry Medhurst was Chelsea's 'man of the match', his bravery and agility almost single-handedly keeping the score within reasonable bounds. It was indeed, as the *Official Programme* commented, 'a sorry start to the New Year', but yet it could have been even worse.

Then, two years later, in March 1950, came two FA Cup semi-final games against Arsenal at White Hart Lane. After 25 minutes of the first game, Chelsea were seemingly striding to victory with Roy Bentley having set up a two-goal lead. But, seconds before half-time, the Arsenal outside-right Freddie Cox hit the second of two corners with the outside of his right foot and the ball, head-high and swerving wickedly, found its way into the net at the near post as Medhurst and a fellow defender desperately failed to stop it.

Arsenal went on to equalise and win the replay.

Poor Harry received criticism from some quarters, but it was more a cruel stroke of fortune which he could do little about.

After a six-month spell at Brighton, Medhurst retired as a player when he was 36, returning to Chelsea as trainer and physiotherapist for a further 15 years. A loyal and highly popular servant, he was succeeded on the training staff by his son, Norman.

Chelsea Career
157 appearances

Tommy Meehan – a live wire full of energy

OCCUPYING a special place in Chelsea history, Tommy Meehan was a regular member in the half-back line for four seasons in the early 1920s.

A Mancurian by birth, he was one of those players whose senior career in the game was postponed by the outbreak of World War One.

He had cut his teeth in the game with such non-League clubs as Newtown, Walkden Central and Rochdale Town, before signing for Manchester United in the summer of 1917 and easing his way on to the Old Trafford stage, making his official debut for the Reds against Sheffield Wednesday on 1 September 1919. He appeared regularly in their team, alternating between wing-half and inside-forward for a season and a half (53 games and six goals) until his transfer to Chelsea in December 1920, for £3,300.

His welcome in *The Chelsea FC Chronicle* (then the title of the club's official programme) was guarded: 'The transfer of Tom Meehan from Manchester United to Chelsea was only accomplished after much negotiation, but the player was always willing, and he will undoubtedly prove an acquisition. Rather on the small side – he stands 5ft 6in and weighs 10st 6lb – Meehan is a "live wire" and is full of energy. He is equally at home in the half-back line and as an inside-forward – and he is a whale on penalty-kicks. Ask Moly!' (Jim Molyneux was Chelsea's goalkeeper in those days.)

Chelsea fans took the little chap to their hearts from the very first. He was a stylish player and both sound defensively and a constructive user of the ball. He won an international cap for England against Ireland in 1924, having played for the Football League representative XI against the Irish League two years earlier.

At the age of 28 he apparently had several more seasons to give Chelsea, so it came as a surprise when his name on the teamsheet was missing early in March 1924. Already relegation to Division Two was threatening (and duly arrived a month later), as the club noted a series of misfortunes 'not the least of which has been the serious illness of Tommy Meehan'.

And then the blow fell. Six months later, and 12 days before Chelsea's opening home fixture on 8 September 1924, Tommy Meehan died. His funeral ceremony was attended by some 2,000 mourners, in torrential rain –"the heavens were not alone in weeping over the loss of a fine fellow" – many of them Chelsea supporters.

Immediately the club opened a fund for his family and relatives (in fact he had two families – his own and his father's to support). He had left four young children and even in life he had been stretched financially.

However, the response was heartwarming. Many sent donations, which were headed by £50 (a considerable sum in those days) from the Football Association, and several other contributions from League clubs up and down the country were also received. Almost £1,500 was the final total.

And, on 20 October 1924, a benefit match was staged at Stamford Bridge with a representative Football League XI providing the opposition.

A wonderful response for a universally popular man.

Chelsea Career

133 appearances   4 goals

Nils Middelboe – Chelsea's Great Dane

ESPECIALLY during their earlier years it was by no means unknown for Chelsea to enlist leading amateur players to join the club and add strength to the first-team whenever available.

Indeed, many will recall the emergence of Seamus O'Connell, the Cumbrian-born inside-forward whose contribution to the 1954–55 Football League championship side was so crucial (seven goals from 10 games).

It was an auspicious day when another of Chelsea's first famous amateurs, Vivian Woodward, introduced the Danish international and Olympic player, Nils Middleboe, to join Chelsea whilst the Dane was working in London.

Woodward had long admired Middleboe's skill and style and after he has approached Woodward for advice on finding him a club in England, the answer was instant: "Come to Chelsea."

And so, on 15 November 1913, Middleboe made his debut for the club, playing at centre-half against Derby County at Stamford Bridge, Chelsea winning the First Division match, 2-1.

He had already proved his pedigree with several outings in the Reserves and effortlessly adapted to the challenge of Football League.

'Our Danish amateur, Nils Middleboe, made quite a sensational debut and more than justified all we wrote about him after witnessing his display with the Reserves,'summarised the programme editor.

After dismissing some of the doubts about Middleboe's apparent lack of pace and a reluctance to commit himself into a tackle, the editor concluded, 'The amateur displayed sound judgement and showed almost unerring intuition in reading the intention of the man with the ball' and summed up, 'In a word, he is particularly brainy half.'

War clouds were gathering, however, and although Middleboe played frequently in the four seasons of unofficial football, it was in the early post-war seasons that he really made his mark, notably in 1919–20 when Chelsea, with 49 points, finished third in the First Division table as well as reaching the semi-final of the FA Cup.

Especially to be recalled was the first Cup-tie of that season, against Bolton Wanderers at Burnden Park, when Chelsea, reduced to nine men – through injury and a sending off – were superbly organised by Middleboe 'who made the team still look as if they were at full strength'.

Stemming the terrific onslaught of the opposition, Chelsea won 1-0.

Middleboe was a keen student of the game with a wide knowledge of its laws. On one occasion, on winning the toss, he told the referee and opposing captain, "We'll kick off," thus surprising both men. But he was quite in order to forego selecting change-of-ends.

Above all, he was a true amateur in every sense of the word.

After joining Chelsea he was asked by the secretary about his expenses. "What expenses?" enquired Middleboe. "I arrived by bus and shall go home on one."

"But let us pay for your lunch and tea," pressed the Chelsea official."

Said Middleboe, "I should have had to take lunch and tea if I hadn't been playing football! Expenses? I ought to pay the club for a fine afternoon's sport."

The Great Dane never lost his affection for Chelsea Football Club and kept in touch with old friends and colleagues. His last appearance was at Wembley in May 1967, when Chelsea played Tottenham Hotspur in the FA Cup Final.

He was an official guest of the club and it was an especially nostalgic occasion for him, renewing old associations. He died in Copenhagen in 1976.

Chelsea Career

46 appearances

Harold Miller – more than just a good clubman

HAROLD Miller was the type of player every manager wishes to have on his staff. He was loyal, reliable, always ready to answer the call and perform whenever required and to occupy whatever position on the field needed him.

However, in 'Dusty's' case there is a danger of remembering him as merely a 'good clubman', whereas he was far more than that.

Many, for example, overlooked the fact that he had represented England against Sweden, in 1923, at the age of 21, soon after he had started his professional career with Charlton Athletic.

Born in St Albans, he was playing with the local club when he first came to the notice of Charlton, who signed him in January 1922. But his time at The Valley lasted only four months or so before Chelsea, two divisions higher in the Football League at that time, snapped him up for a small fee.

And it is reasonable to say that no player in the club's history ever gave better value for money.

At that time, big names who had already established their reputation were regularly enticed to Stamford Bridge, some failing to live up to expectation, and others merely proving birds of passage.

None, though, were more loyal, or more dependable, than Miller.

His first 10 seasons or so were spent mainly in the forward line, at inside-left; his role to open up defences and lay on scoring chances for the series of better-known strikers such as Bob Turnbull, Jim Thompson, Hughie Gallacher and George Mills.

Then latterly, he moved back to wing-half, where his sound positional play intercepted enemy raids and his shrewd use of the ball set his own attackers in motion.

Essentially he was a left-footed player, possessing considerable skill with the ball and also with delicate footwork and artistry. For one of such slight build, his strength in the tackle surprised many a weightier opponent.

Although his tally of less than 50 goals over 15 seasons may seem a meagre return, this is largely explained by the variety of different roles he occupied.

But in the 1929–30 season, playing in a more advanced position, he scored 13 times, only one fewer than centre-forward George Mills.

Most of his goals were the result of his skill and accuracy from close range. Few were the result of powerful long-range shooting. Rather he had the ability to defeat opposing goalkeepers with pin-point placement.

He served two managers, both of whom could not always find a place for him in the first team. But each knew where to turn in moments of crisis. And neither was ever let down.

At the age of 37, his days at First Division level were over and in May 1939 he signed for Northampton Town on a free transfer. He played only three games for the Cobblers before war was declared when he finally hung up his boots.

Chelsea Career

363 appearances   44 goals

George Mills – something of an enigma

ONE of the longest serving and most loyal servants in Chelsea's history, George Mills was yet something of an enigma.

Born in Deptford he was playing local football for Bromley when he signed amateur forms for Chelsea in December 1929.

Tall and well-built, he arrived at Stamford Bridge as a somewhat gangly youth, yet within days was to demonstrate his potential and ability as a natural goalscorer.

Almost immediately good fortune presented Mills with the perfect opportunity to prove himself. Four days before Christmas 1929, Chelsea defeated Preston North End by five clear goals at Stamford Bridge and Mills made his debut.

Throughout that season goalscoring was never a problem as Chelsea won promotion back to the First Division after a five-year absence.

But, on Boxing Day, an injury to the regular centre-forward provided Mills with another unexpected opportunity to show his potential and he responded immediately by scoring in Chelsea's 4-0 victory

Two months later, and still spending the weekdays at his office desk in the City, further injuries gave Mills a real chance which he grasped. A run of 16 consecutive games brought him 13 goals.

Yet still the management were not convinced and before the next season started they had signed the most famous centre-forward in Britain at that time, Hughie Gallacher.

Not until the following New Year did Mills receive another chance in First Division football. There were times when he figured at inside-right but it was as leader of the attack that his talents were best displayed.

Gallacher's departure in December 1934 appeared to leave the centre-forward position for Mills to at last stake his undisputed claim, but within weeks the management had seen fit to sign the Irish international Joe Bambrick, who immediately justified his place by scoring goals regularly. Mills, meanwhile, made only one further appearance in the last 20 games.

Patience and loyalty, however, were ultimately rewarded when, in the 1937–38 season and nine years after joining the Chelsea staff, George Mills was selected to play for England, against Ireland, Wales and Czechoslovakia. After a long wait he enjoyed a remarkable debut, scoring a hat-trick against the Irish.

Not until November 1936 had Mills become Chelsea's undisputed first-choice centre-forward; and he responded with 22 goals in 32 games.

His worth had been belatedly recognised. Mills' talents were obvious for all to appreciate. Standing 6ft tall, his strong physical presence was matched by a big heart and skilful ball control.

When World War Two began, Mills was past his 30th birthday and Joe Payne, who had scored 10 goals for Luton Town in a Football League fixture two years previously, had edged George out of the limelight once more.

A handful of games at the beginning of the war and he was gone, his final appearance coming in October 1941, by which time he had returned to the printing trade from which he had been lured 12 years previously.

But, not quite gone. Football remained in his blood. A hobby. And when normal football resumed in 1946, George Mills reappeared, travelling with the Chelsea 'A' team youngsters, passing on words of advice and wisdom.

He died, aged 70, in the summer of 1978, having attended first-team games at Stamford Bridge almost to the end of his life.

Chelsea Career

239 appearances   123 goals

James Molyneux – a bloomin' hero all his days

FROM the moment the ample frame of Willie Foulke – all 22st of him – filled a substantial part of the space between the two goalposts at Stockport in Chelsea's first-ever League fixture, in September 1905, to the present day, with the slim, athletic Carlo Cudicini as the last line of defence, the club has been well-served in its goalkeepers.

Around a dozen international 'keepers have played for Chelsea down the years, with many others also of high quality, even if they did not represent their countries.

In August 1910, at the start of Chelsea's sixth season, and with the club finding themselves back in the Second Division after experiencing relegation for the first time, a fee of £550 had been paid to Stockport County for their 23-year-old goalkeeper, James Molyneux.

Immediately he won his place in the first team, making his debut against Derby County at the Baseball Ground.

Seven days later, following a 4-1 victory at Derby, the *Official Programme* scribe contented himself by saying somewhat quaintly, 'In J. Molyneux. late of Stockport County, we have what I regard as a capture.' The writer went on almost apologetically to justify the replacement of his predecessor, Jack Whitley, who in fact went on to stay at the club, on the training staff, for a further 29 years.

In addition he was at pains to point out that Molyneux had conceded only 47 goals during the previous season, despite Stockport occupying a lowly place in the table.

Be that as it may, Molyneux firmly established himself as Chelsea's first-choice in goal, missing only one League game, through injury.

Apart from one period, he retained this position almost unchallenged until the outbreak of World War One, his appearances interrupted only by the presence in London of a north country dental student, Ronald Brebner, who won 23 amateur international caps for England.

In the final season before war closed down normal football in April 1915, Chelsea fought their way to the FA Cup Final, against Sheffield United, a game played at Old Trafford for 'security reasons'.

Having conceded only four goals in the seven Cup-ties leading to the Final, Chelsea were outplayed, losing by three goals, the first of which resulted from an uncharacteristic fumble on the part of Molyneux.

Away for the rest of the war, 'Sunlight Jim' as he was known, resumed his place in September 1919. During hostilities he had enlisted in the Royal Field Artillery because, as he put it, "I've being stopping shots for years and wanted to give the blue-eyed disciples of 'kultur' something to stop on my own!"

Certainly he was in the thick of the war, or as be put it, "A bit exciting at times but nothing much out of the way after keeping goal." He was being modest, for he had stopped a piece of shrapnel which finished his career as a gunner.

Nevertheless he was back at his peacetime post for the resumption of normal football. Age, of course, was creeping up and in October 1921 he was replaced in the Chelsea goal by the colourful amateur, Benjamin Howard Baker, whereupon Molyneux returned to Stockport to wind down his long playing career with County.

He could look back on winning one medal with Chelsea – in the 3-0 London Victory Cup Final against Fulham, at Highbury.

He was not only a goalkeeper but something of a philosopher too.

Always with a fund of good humour, and the idol of supporters, especially the younger ones, he once said in the dressing room after a heavy defeat, "Win a game one Saturday and you're a bloomin' hero; get beat the next and everybody shouting. Never mind, that's a footballer's life all over."

Chelsea Career

239 appearances

John Mortimore – guiding Docherty's ducklings

IN the days when some amateur players were good enough to play in the Football League, it was customary to differentiate them from professionals by including an initial before the surname.

Thus, in the final fixture of the 1955–56 season, replacing the regular left-half was 'J. Mortimore'. This was announced over the public address system and to most of the 35,000 crowd it meant little or nothing, although the debutant had previously made two appearances in the Combination team.

Only the more knowledgeable would have known that the player had won English youth and amateur recognition whilst at Woking.

It was clear from the very beginning that Mortimore, like manager Ted Drake's several other recruits from the unpaid ranks, would make the transition without difficulty and, in John's case, despite the fact that he was midway through a teacher-training course.

This was the reason he appeared only twice in Chelsea's League side the following season, after which he played regularly in the first-team.

"I was studying Craft, PE, Maths, and Geography and manager Ted Drake agreed that I should be allowed to complete my studies."

And it was worth the waiting as Mortimore immediately proved from August 1957 onwards.

Only Peter Sillett and Derek Saunders remained as regulars from the championship team of two seasons earlier. And while Jimmy Greaves was bursting on the scene, there were several other young players, some of whom ultimately never made the grade, but who needed an experienced hand at the tiller.

Mortimore, even though himself new to the professional game, was an excellent tutor.

He was a towering figure in defence, commanding in the air and always mindful of the importance of constructively using the ball from the back.

Probably the peak of his Stamford Bridge career was the promotion season of 1962–63 when, after one year in Division Two, he piloted Tommy Docherty's new team (his 'ducklings'), heavily reliant on youth, back to the top class. That season John Mortimore was ever present.

Two years later he was still at the helm when Chelsea won the Football League Cup, and he was now the senior citizen in the team, unflappable and totally in charge.

The following summer he moved down the road to Queen's Park Rangers for an £8,000 fee. But injury, and the realisation that his future now lay more in coaching, virtually ended his days as a player. After suffering a triple fracture of the jaw during a match at Loftus Road, he knew it was time to go.

"I felt that I must be slowing up to get caught like that. Tommy Docherty had helped me to make a start in coaching and recommended me to Sunderland where I had two valuable years in that capacity."

Having been appointed assistant-manager of Southampton in 1971, he later had two spells coaching in Greece, was manager-coach of Benfica in Portugal (also in two spells) as well as taking up an assignment in Spain. He managed Portsmouth in 1973-74.

Thereafter, his second home became Southampton as he returned there to serve the Saints in a variety of capacities and always remembered by older Chelsea supporters on their annual visit to Hampshire.

He was happy to discuss the old days, and the infamous refereeing decision in an FA Cup semi-final against Liverpool, when his clean header from a corner found the net, but was mysteriously disallowed, almost certainly denying Chelsea a Wembley Final.

Chelsea Career

279 appearances   10 goals

Pat Nevin – ...but what a genius!

THE summer of 1983 can fairly be described as a watershed in the history of Chelsea FC.

At the beginning of May the prospect of relegation into the Third Division had been very real and was avoided only after a desperate and undignified struggle.

Manager John Neal welcomed supporters to the first game of the following season. "We haven't been sitting on our backsides during the summer... for with tremendous drive from the chairman and backroom staff here I've been able to sign a number of players at considerable cost."

And the new boys included Eddie Niedzwiecki, Joe McLaughlin, Nigel Spackman, Kerry Dixon and Pat Nevin, along with old boys Alan Hudson and John Hollins who both returned to the fold.

By the time that the first-day crowd streamed away from Stamford Bridge, opponents Derby County were licking their wounds, having lost 5-0.

Strangely, Pat Nevin had not been included in that team, his debut, as substitute, coming two weeks later.

But once the 20-year-old from Clyde appeared, in a League Cup-tie against Gillingham, he was never going to be overlooked.

And, indeed, as Chelsea romped away to promotion, Nevin played in every subsequent fixture.

His total mastery of the ball, his mazy dribbles and acceleration away from leaden-footed opponents, and his precision passing, would have brought him fame for those qualities alone. But, in addition to being a creator of chances for such as Dixon and David Speedie, he was himself a prolific goalscorer.

Probably the best remembered display of his genius at Chelsea came with an amazing 80-yard dribble against Newcastle United at the Bridge, in his first season.

"It was in the first half," Nevin recalled years later. "I tackled someone in our box, which was astounding in itself, and then set off. I never really had it in mind to dribble that far. People kept expecting me to pass but I held the ball out of necessity because there was never a pass on. I just kept going and crossed it instead."

As one scribe put it, "Pat Nevin must have dribbled past at least 20 Newcastle players on that run!"

Another trait was his liking to hold the ball and attract opponents round him, as a magnet attracts metal, before weaving his was past and, seemingly through them, just as Stanley Matthews had done years before.

And no one since Dick Spence, in an earlier age, had exceeded in Pat's goalscoring output for a winger.

Off the field, and away from the Fulham Road, he made the best of his time in London, pursuing many interests, not all of them normally in a footballer's repertoire. Museums, art galleries, the theatre – all consumed the leisure hours of this most articulate and friendly man.

In 1985–86, Nevin was Chelsea's Player of the Year. Making the presentation, chairman Ken Bates jokingly remarked, "Pat Nevin. He is a weirdo. Reads classical novels, listens to way-out music and dresses at Oxfam. But what a genius!"

When he moved to Everton for a £925,000 fee, in July 1988 – and still only 25 – it was a blow to his army of fans in SW6. And then, later, after a spell with Tranmere Rovers, he returned north of the border to Motherwell, serving that club in a variety of capacities, both on and off the field, and experiencing European football for the first time.

Hopefully, the game has not yet heard the last of Pat Nevin. Football needs such thinkers to steer it into its future, drawing on playing experience as well as contributing to discussions at the conference table.

Chelsea Career

237-5 appearances   45 goals

Eddie Niedzwiecki – expert in the art of goalkeeping

IT was in May 1983 that Eddie Niedzwiecki arrived at Stamford Bridge, following one of the darkest seasons in Chelsea's history, and became part of a major rebuilding programme.

The Welshman was a goalkeeper of the highest class and only the continued brilliance of Neville Southall confined his appearances in the national team to a miserly two caps.

From the opening fixture of his first season at the Bridge he radiated the confidence, which had been missing, into those in front of him.

He dominated his penalty area, coming unhesitatingly and with confidence for crosses; his long arms plucking the ball from the sky as opposing attackers challenged in vain. He was brave and, for a big man, he showed extraordinary agility as in his first season Chelsea simply romped away to promotion. Never once was Niedzwiecki absent from his post.

And he went on to miss only two games out of a possible 140 before, for the first time, he was struck down by injury.

It was in a League fixture against Queen's Park Rangers in March 1986 at Stamford Bridge. His left knee was badly damaged and major surgery was required.

And it was not until the following November that he was able to resume. It appeared straight away that Niedzwiecki would take time to shake off the full affects of the problem, and after a mere 13 first-team games it was back to hospital after once more breaking down at Norwich.

"I can honestly say that I wasn't fit in any of those games," confessed the big man afterwards.

"It was hard because it was a season in which I hoped the injury would have got better. It didn't, and eventually we learned that a piece of cartilage had torn and got round the knee to cause discomfort."

Ten little bits of the cartilage were removed and so it was back to breaking through the pain barrier once more.

For the second time Niedzwiecki began to re-establish his career and he started the 1987–88 season optimistically, hoping at last to attain 100 per cent fitness.

Wales, too, shared this confidence and within three weeks of his latest comeback named him in their international squad. It seemed, too, as if he might well be required to play as Southall was ill at the time. But it was during a training section with the national squad that it was noticed Eddie was still limping whilst running.

Sensibly, the Welsh FA were not prepared to take the risk of selecting him (not least for insurance reasons), and in any case Southall recovered in time to play.

For another eight weeks or so Niedzwiecki soldiered on, playing 14 consecutive games for Chelsea. But then, on 31 October 1987, his career finally ended at Oxford United.

With less than 10 minutes to go, he came off his line to make a routine catch. Having collected the ball, the big man the collapsed in pain and was forced to leave the field.

"As I landed, my knee sort of twisted the other way," he reported. "I'll go and see the surgeon who operated before and we will take it from there. I'll just have to keep my fingers crossed, and say a few prayers, and hope for the best."

'Nothing seriously wrong' was the verdict but, nevertheless, Eddie Niedzwiecki never played again.

He moved into coaching at Stamford Bridge, with the youth team, had an 18-month spell at Reading as Ian Porterfield's assistant, and then came back on the Chelsea coaching staff with Porterfield in 1991, as goalkeeping and reserve-team coach, later concentrating solely with the 'keepers for some six years.

Eddie Niedzwiecki is still actively involved in the game as a highly respected authority on the art of goalkeeping.

Chelsea Career
175 appearances

Seamus O'Connell – Englishman with an Irish name

AT the beginning of the 1954–55 season, Chelsea manager Ted Drake signed an English amateur international forward from the North-East. At the time it aroused little interest and, after almost seven weeks of the campaign had passed, it seemed as if he had been forgotten, never even having travelled to London, let alone pulled on a blue shirt.

Born of Irish parents, Seamus O'Connell had twice played for the England Amateur XI, helped Bishop Auckland to reach Wembley in the FA Amateur Cup Final, and played for Queen's Park in the Scottish League and also made three Football League appearances for Middlesbrough (scoring two goals) prior to arriving at Stamford Bridge.

Contrary to information in the club's history books, he made his debut for Chelsea against Brentford at Griffin Park on 5 October 1954, in a friendly match to mark the switching on of the Bees' first floodlights.

O'Connell's name did not appear on the team listed in the match programme and although Chelsea cantered to an easy 4-0 win, surprisingly, in view of his later exploits, neither did he figure on the scoresheet.

Yet he certainly impressed Drake who, after another first-team friendly at Hull, then selected him for a crucial First Division home game against Manchester United five days later, introducing him in the programme with the words, 'The greatest satisfaction of all to me at Hull was the successful introduction of the popular Amateur International, Seamus O'Connell.

'He did so well that you will have the opportunity of seeing him in action this afternoon. Welcome to Stamford Bridge, Seamus, and may we see you often!'

By Saturday evening on that day Seamus O'Connell was the name on everyone's lips. A 55,000 crowd had watched spellbound as 11 goals were scored, with United winning an extraordinary game 6-5. Nevertheless the spotlight was firmly focussed on O'Connell who scored a memorable hat-trick.

With Chelsea already trailing by three goals, he reduced the deficit with a powerful drive from 20 yards, was then on hand to tap in Chelsea's fourth in a storming fight-back, before putting a rebound off the crossbar into the net with 14 minutes remaining which, in view of what had gone before, surprisingly passed without a further goal.

As Drake said afterwards "Nothing quite as remarkable has ever been seen at Stamford Bridge in a lifetime."

By the end of that historic season, O'Connell, sharing the inside-left position with Les Stubbs, scored seven goals in 10 League games and was in the side when the Football League championship was won on 9 April 1954. Thereafter he played another half a dozen games for Chelsea in the following season. But, ambition satisfied and appetite gone, he never came to Stamford Bridge again.

As his record suggests, goalscoring was his greatest asset. Well-built, he was a fine mover with the ball yet it remains something of a mystery why he turned his back on the game at the age of 25, apart from later very occasional appearances for Crook Town and Carlisle United.

Rather, he devoted his attention to helping his father in the cattle-dealing business.

A notable absentee from the periodic reunions of the 1954–55 Chelsea championship heroes, he retired to savour the Spanish sunshine and live with his soccer memories.

Chelsea Career

17 appearances   12 goals

Peter O'Dowd – the club's greatest centre-half?

THE name of Peter O'Dowd rarely receives a mention in Chelsea's history today.

Yet those who saw his somewhat fleeting days with the club were in no doubt whatsoever that he was the greatest centre-half up to that time.

Born in Halifax, after playing with Bradford for a spell as an amateur, he turned professional with Blackburn Rovers where he developed and made 50 first-team appearances, mostly at wing-half, in three seasons before moving down the road to Burnley where he was an automatic first-team choice in a brief stay of just over 12 months.

So great an impression did he make that Chelsea paid £5,250 for his services in November 1931, an unusually large sum for a defender in those days.

Standing just under 6ft tall, O'Dowd had a commanding presence and played the game with no apparent effort, strolling around in defence with a casual air and time to dwell on the ball and launch an attack.

In fact, despite appearances, he was deceptively quick, not least mentally. He had a superb footballing brain.

He broke on to the representative football scene in the FA tour to Canada in the summer of 1931, returning with glowing reports of his performances.

Burnley's financial problems, however, were Chelsea's gain and the Lancashire club found it impossible to refuse what was then a generous offer.

O'Dowd's first-team debut for his new club, against Everton at Goodison Park, was scarcely auspicious. Inspired by a five-star performance from Dixie Dean, the Merseysiders won 7-2 with Dixie claiming five goals himself.

Better days, however, were swift in arriving. Within months of his arrival at Stamford Bridge O'Dowd won his first international cap for England, against Scotland at Wembley. One reporter summed up the 3-0 victory, 'To Peter O'Dowd, more than any other player, did England owe their success'.

An England selector went further. "O'Dowd is not a policeman; he is a football player. He does not hang about in the goalmouth but goes up with the play, all the time helping his forwards. It may be all right for some clubs to have a purely defensive centre-half but it isn't what the FA want and why I am sure he will play for England for many years.

"Sometimes you think he hasn't a million-to-one chances of getting back to stop an attack. Yet he walks there and clears."

Unfortunately, and surely inadvisedly, Chelsea didn't see it that way. They saw him only as a stopper centre-half. And although he tried to obey instructions it simply wasn't his game and he had to follow instinct.

He received two further international caps, against Ireland and Switzerland, before asking Chelsea for a transfer and crossing the Channel to sign for Valenciennes for £3,000, becoming the first England player for whom a French club paid a transfer fee.

Before leaving Stamford Bridge, O'Dowd had been taken ill on a Chelsea trip to Berlin. Then still feeling unwell and unable to play to instructions, almost unbelievably, he was relegated to the reserve side.

After three seasons across the Channel he returned to England and, at the age of only 29, signed for the Third Division South club Torquay United, where he ended his playing career.

He was something of a mystery man, a problem player for a manager. Wherever he went he failed to settle, allowing his extraordinary gifts never to be properly exploited or used for any length of time.

Chelsea Career

87 appearances

Peter Osgood – answer to a manager's prayers

'PETER Osgood is one of those natural players a manager hopes and prays for throughout his career but so rarely are his prayers answered.' So wrote Tommy Docherty, Chelsea's manager, when Osgood first burst on the scene.

From the moment he arrived at Stamford Bridge, his outstanding gifts were apparent and news of his skills spread rapidly as a result of his deeds in the juniors.

Before his 18th birthday he had made his first-team debut, in a Football League Cup-tie replay in December 1964, against Workington at Stamford Bridge, the newcomer scoring both goals in Chelsea's 2-0 victory.

He made the transition into League football instantly, so easy and so naturally, everything achieved with a casual, almost disinterested air.

He revelled in the big occasions against top opposition and in front of large crowds. Not so attractive for him were those wet, inhospitable winter's evenings on smaller grounds in northern outposts.

Probably no one has scored more memorable goals for Chelsea down the years. That crucial diving header in the 1970 FA Cup Final replay at Old Trafford, followed just over 12 months later by two more in the contest with Real Madrid in the European Cup-winners' Cup Final in Athens.

At Stamford Bridge his goal against AC Milan in a Fairs' Cup-tie will never be forgotten by the near 60,000 present in 1966, nor indeed will a similar vintage strike in an FA Cup-tie against Arsenal seven years later.

Every Chelsea follower of Ozzie's Chelsea's days will have their own recollections of his extraordinary skills and panache for the big occasions. And goals set up, and finished by him.

Sadly, this talent was all too rarely paraded on the international stage. If Docherty was the ideal manager for Peter, Sir Alf Ramsay most certainly was not, and was sadly not prepared to accommodate his individuality and, at times, refusal to conform both on and off the field.

As Peter himself put it, "He wants hard work, lots of effort. Players who will run for each other, challenge back for the ball if they lose it. I'd very much like to play that way. But I can't. I've tried."

And so while men of lesser ability were called up to the colours, Osgood retired with a mere four England caps to his name.

Docherty's successor, Dave Sexton, also found it difficult to tune in to his extravagant lifestyle and fell out with him, as indeed he did with other senior professionals.

The bright lights of the King's Road, as well as Stamford Bridge, formed an essential part of Osgood's life and, as a result, Sexton admitted defeat and allowed one of Chelsea's all-time greats to move, to Southampton.

The curtain was coming down on the greatest days in Chelsea FC's history up to that time.

Then, the final postscript. Soon Sexton had also been ushered out of the door and, after three other incumbents in the managerial chair had failed to remedy declining fortunes, Danny Blanchflower was appointed to take charge in December 1978.

Almost at once he re-signed Peter Osgood to return to the stage on which he had performed his greatest acts. And although Blanchflower might well have been an ideal leader and kindred spirit for Osgood in his prime, now it didn't work.

At the age of 31, and with increased girth, the pace, and the magic, had gone. Ten more games, at somewhat irregular intervals, and for the second, and final, time the curtain fell on one of Chelsea's greatest players. Ever.

Chelsea Career

376-4 appearances   150 goals

Eric Parsons – few made a greater impact

WITHOUT doubt Chelsea manager Ted Drake was one of the most shrewd operators in the transfer market that the club has had. Virtually the whole of his 1954–55 championship team was drawn from the lower divisions or the amateur ranks, Roy Bentley whom he inherited being the only outstanding exception.

And few made a greater impact than Eric Parsons. After five seasons and 150 senior games for West Ham United in the Second Division. Drake sensed that the little winger was not making the best use of his talents.

Initially he lacked self-confidence and much of his first two seasons were spent in the reserve team.

Then, in the 1953–54 campaign, it all started to come together. As his self-belief returned, he became the darling of the fans who nicknamed him 'the Rabbit'. Apparently finding an extra yard or two of pace, he would zip down the right wing, ridding himself of the attention of opponents before presenting goalscoring opportunities pin-pointed on to the head, or feet, of Roy Bentley.

Parsons scored 42 goals in 177 games but his contribution to the team in other ways cannot be measured in mere statistics.

"Being in the championship side was the biggest thing I achieved in football", he said. "And the years I spent at Chelsea were the best of my career – a big club with a lot of style. Everything was first-class."

In that championship season his output of goals before the final home fixture, against Sheffield Wednesday was nine from 40 League fixtures, already equalling the best of his career.

But on Saturday, 23 April, the day that the title was won, he scored twice in Chelsea's vital 3-0 win.

And, after the final whistle, and the speeches had been delivered to the vast crowd assembled in front of the directors' box, Eric Parsons, who had been sitting astride the front ledge, suddenly became their special hero of the day.

Over and again the chant rang out, "We want the Rabbit." Totally unable to hide his embarrassment, Eric could find no escape, but, if words never came, he acknowledged the fans' acclaim with a dignified bow before finally running off with almost as much haste as he used to defeat opponents on the pitch.

It was his greatest day and, of course, also one of Chelsea's most famous occasions, too.

Parsons played on for another full season at Stamford Bridge before winding down his career with Brentford (for four years) and Dover (for another three) where he helped them win the Kent League title.

In retirement his sporting instincts turned him to bowls where he won the English singles and pairs, as well as numerous other local events.

A true competitor and a popular and most engaging character.

Attending reunions of the championship team, more than 40 years on, Eric Parsons looked as fit as ever, the mischievous glint in his eyes showing that his zest for life had in no way diminished.

Chelsea Career

177 appearances   42 goals

Dan Petrescu – one of our own

FROM the day he signed for Chelsea, from Sheffield Wednesday in November 1995, aged 28, Dan Petrescu became a Londoner. He loved the place and he loved Chelsea and everything in the club. All sentiments which were echoed by his wife.

Chelsea was his sixth club, after Steaua Bucharest, Olt (on loan), Foggia, Genoa and Wednesday.

And if he loved Chelsea, the club's fans certainly loved Dan, immediately claiming him as one of their own. Indeed, as his Stamford Bridge career drew to its close – prematurely many thought – on more than one occasion he refused to leave, so great was his affinity with the place.

Signed by Glenn Hoddle for £2.3 million (equalling the club record at that time) he was a wonderful buy.

Essentially a right-sided player, he could operate to great effect as a right-back, right wing-back or on the right side of midfield, accelerating forward at high speed accompanied by the loud vocal encouragement from his army of fans.

His philosophy was simple: "Keep the ball moving, to keep the team moving and let the opposition find the ball – if they can."

Of course, his regular contribution of goals was a bonus.

Glenn Hoddle's 'beautiful game' philosophy was an ideal scenario for Petrescu and, he possibly more than anyone else, along with Ruud Gullit, achieved that ambition.

Later on Ruud himself, Hoddle's successor in the managerial seat, could not always find a place for Petrescu in the first team. He had opportunities to move on, but several times refused such offers. As a result he contributed to several more notable achievements.

By the time he left Stamford Bridge he had won more international caps (44) than anyone else in Chelsea's history at that time. He was the first overseas player to chalk up more than 200 appearances (a feat for which he received a special presentation) and, of course, he won three Cup-winners' medals – in the FA Cup, Football League Cup and European Cup-winners' Cup.

These added to his previous tally of four Romanian League championship medals and two Romanian FA Cup winners' prior to his arrival in England.

The longer his career in the Premiership progressed the more he felt that he was becoming a marked man. When he arrived he was able to express himself. – "They didn't care about me". Later he was subjected to close man-marking. It was a compliment maybe, but one which did not make life easier.

Petrescu was a perfectionist and a most dedicated professional. Always one of the last to leave the training pitch, he would have a brief lunch break and then follow this with a hard stint in the gym.

Reluctantly, in the spring of 2000 it was time for him to move. Even though he was approaching his 34th birthday, Bradford City valued his services at £1 million.

It was an emotional parting of the ways. "I've had five wonderful years at Chelsea; the best five years in my life. And you know that Chelsea will always be in my heart for all my life."

Chelsea Career

186-22 appearances   23 goals

Gustavo Poyet – the complete midfielder

IT was in the semi-final of the European Cup-winners' Cup in 1995 that Uruguayan Gustavo Poyet first came to the notice of Chelsea, when he was playing for Real Zaragoza.

No fewer than three Chelsea scouts, quite independently, had specially singled him out when sizing up the opposition prior to the game itself.

Poyet had begun his playing career with River Plate, in his home town of Montevideo, before joining Zaragoza, via spells with Grenoble and Bellavista.

The complete midfield player, he had fine skills and a wonderful technique. On the ball his class shone through and his height (6ft 2in) made him dominant in aerial combat. Indeed he was an inspiration to those around him.

Another asset was his versatility. If midfield was his best position and most influential sphere of operation, he could also slot into the centre-back position in emergency and, of course, his regular output of goals – many of them scored at crucial moments – was an enormous bonus. In his last four seasons in Spanish football he had scored 47 times, a contribution most forwards would be proud to claim.

At Chelsea many of his 40-plus goals arrived at opportune moments as he surged forward from midfield, often rising to meet crosses and flashing the ball into the net with bullet-force headers.

Aged 30, he came to Chelsea on a free transfer and, despite suffering setbacks with injuries, made his mark immediately. In fact, a popular opinion was that if Gustavo had remained fit in his first season, then the Premiership championship might well have come to Stamford Bridge. And the failure to win this particular medal was probably his greatest disappointment during his days at the Bridge.

More than most he found inactivity when injured hard to accept. Watching Chelsea win the Football League Cup Final against Middlesbrough at Wembley in March 1998, was particularly aggravating.

"It was nice to see the game and very important for Chelsea to win. But for me I don't do anything and I want to help. Perhaps next time I can do more. The Final maybe. If not, then next season for sure."

And, of course, his wish came true when he was a member of the side which won the FA Cup against Aston Villa at Wembley in May 2000. It was a triumph made possible, not least, by Poyet scoring both goals in the 2-1 semi-final victory against Newcastle United (also at Wembley). One a delightful chip and the other a header.

Frustratingly he left Stamford Bridge with two of his main ambitions unrealised Not only the lack of a League championship medal (he never stopped talking about it) but also not appearing in a World Cup finals for Uruguay.

It was a blow to his vast army of fans at Stamford Bridge when his contract was not renewed at the end of the 2000–01 season, when he was 33. It was a disappointment in no way made more acceptable when he threw in his lot with Tottenham Hotspur. Such was his lasting popularity that he nevertheless still received a warm welcome on his return visits to the Bridge.

Chelsea Career

110-35 appearances   49 goals

Graham Roberts – man of steel

A MAN of steel, Graham Roberts was a hard, uncompromising player, either in defence or midfield.

Tottenham Hotspur had signed him from Weymouth in May 1980, for £35,000, then the highest fee ever paid for a non-League player.

And, indeed, his greatest days were spent at White Hart Lane where he won two FA Cup winners' medals and a UEFA Cup winners' medal in 1984.

Then, moving north of the border to Glasgow Rangers, he added a League Cup-winners' medal to his collection during a stay of two years.

He arrived at Stamford Bridge in August 1988 and was soon appointed captain. Immediately his powerful presence and aggression gave the team the leadership and example which had been missing for some time. Chelsea romped away with the Second Divisions championship.

Not least was his contribution of 15 goals, mostly from the penalty spot. They were an important bonus.

One of his most vivid memories of that season was the game against West Bromwich Albion at Stamford Bridge in December.

"Albion were our closest rivals and they had taken an early lead. After that we dominated without scoring; the ball just wouldn't go in. Then a harmless looking cross was pushed away by the hands of a defender.

"It was a crucial moment, but I wasn't nervous. I had to walk the length of the pitch, but I knew exactly where I was going to put it."

Roberts scored. Chelsea won a vital point, and stayed on top of the table.

Above all, he was the right man at the right time to come to Chelsea and he turned out to be probably manager Bobby Campbell's best-ever signing.

He set standards which, in recent times, had been all-too-often missing. His very presence instilled confidence. His enthusiasm rubbed off on those around him. And, above all, he immediately won the respect of Chelsea's entire professional staff.

For Graham, who had already reached the high point in his profession and had six England caps to his name, it was a new challenge which, at the age of 29, he was ready to meet.

In his first season Chelsea dominated the Second Division, finishing 17 points above runners-up Manchester City. Only five games (out of 46) were lost, three of them in the first six games, as, increasingly, it became a one-horse race.

And Roberts never regretted his move back to London.

"I've enjoyed it," he said as Chelsea's success took them to the top. "We started a little shakily after going down last season, but everyone worked hard in training and on the field, and the manager has always believed in us."

For one more season Roberts was a linchpin of Chelsea's defence, helping the team to take the greater challenge of the First Division in their stride; they finished in fifth place in the table.

Then, in November 1990, and at the age of 31, he signed for West Bromwich Albion for a fee of £200,000.

By then his lack of pace was being exposed and his appointment on the Chelsea coaching staff had led to problems over contractual obligations.

He had found the transition from his former role none too easy. As he said, "Although they've kicked me out of the players' dressing room. I'm still just a member of the team on Saturdays." But it wasn't the same.

And so he had to have his appetite again satisfied – on the field.

Chelsea Career

83 appearances   22 goals

Derek Saunders – one of a select band

ONE of that select band which manager Ted Drake recruited from amateur football to make the transition to the highest level in the professional game, the English First Division, Derek Saunders played in all 42 Football League games in Chelsea's championship team of 1954–55.

Already an English amateur international and playing for Walthamstow Avenue, he came to Stamford Bridge during the summer of 1953.

"I was working as a shipping clerk, not far from Stamford Bridge, when Ted invited me to sign professional and the move worked out very well."

Apart from his amateur international caps, Saunders had represented Great Britain in the 1952 Helsinki Olympics and, understandably, was keen to test his ability at an even higher level in the game.

In fact he took the step up easily and without fuss.

At left-half, and playing in front of Stan Willemse for three seasons, the pair of them presented a solid and fearsome barrier down this side of Chelsea's defensive flank.

Saunders was a strong, physical presence, tackling opponents with, as one writer put it, 'fire to match his red hair'.

But if he is especially remembered for his defensive solidarity, it would be remiss to overlook the more constructive side of his game.

His range of passing, mostly from his left foot, was considerable, often finding Eric Parsons on the opposite wing, 60 yards distant, with accurate balls, and prising open opposition defences.

For his last two seasons at Stamford Bridge, Saunders was appointed captain. Then a senior professional, he provided a wise tutor to the steady influx of youngsters – 'Drake's Ducklings' – emerging from the youth scheme, before injury ended his playing career at the age of 31.

He remained at Stamford Bridge, on the coaching side, for a period before taking up an appointment at Westminster School as football coach and groundsman.

Not that football was everything in his life; he was also tutor-in-charge of Putney and Wandsworth Adult Education with the Inner London Education Authority.

Like other colleagues who treasure a Football League championship medal, he remembers one game in that 1954–55 season above all others, the Easter Saturday fixture with Wolves at Stamford Bridge.

"It was going to be us or them and we won with that penalty we nearly didn't get. The referee hadn't seen what happened but fortunately the linesman had and Peter Sillett nearly broke the net with his shot. What a moment!"

Chelsea Career

223 appearances   9 goals

Ken Shellito – a great communicator

WITH just over 100 first-team games for Chelsea, the name of Ken Shellito will never figure as largely in the club's history as the ability and skill he possessed entitles him to.

He joined Chelsea as a junior in 1955, aged 15, and at once showed that he possessed all the attributes to reach the top of his profession.

By giving him his senior debut a few days before his 19th birthday, against Nottingham Forest at the City Ground, his first Stamford Bridge manager, Ted Drake, showed that the teenager figured prominently in his long-term plans.

But it was Tommy Docherty, taking over as chief coach in October 1961, who really gave Shellito his head. Replacing John Sillett at right-back, Shellito retained his place in what was a difficult and depressing season as Chelsea nose-dived into relegation to the Second Division, finishing at the foot of the table with only 28 points.

In fact Shellito's full-back partnership with the Scot, Eddie McCreadie, was one of the few bright spots and it continued to flourish as Chelsea stormed their way to promotion 12 months later, with both men en route to recognition by their respective international selectors.

Shellito, perhaps lacking a little in pace, nevertheless compensated both with his sound positional play and his ability to read the game. Rarely could a winger claim to have got the better of this solid right-back who nudged the scales at almost 13st.

In addition to such qualities, Shellito's passing out from the back was an important feature of his play, tutored by his manager who placed much emphasis on building attacks from deep positions. His accuracy and long-distance use of the ball were an additional asset.

The influence of Docherty's coach, Dave Sexton – later to himself become manager – was an obvious influence as he encouraged the overlapping runs of both full-backs.

Sadly, that was to be their only complete season in partnership together.

Having won his only international cap, for England against Czechoslovakia on the summer tour of 1963, Shellito injured his left knee in a home fixture against Sheffield Wednesday the following October and, although he returned to first-team duty five months later, it was obvious that all was not well.

It was merely a prelude to a series of prolonged visits to the surgeon and hospitalisation, involving four cartilage operations. Never again was he truly fit.

Courage and determination were simply not enough for his career to be permanently resurrected, his final appearance in a Chelsea shirt coming in a Fairs' Cup-tie against the Austrian side, Wiener Sports Club, on 1 December 1965, leaving one to contemplate what heights he might have scaled had the fates smiled on him.

He continued to serve Chelsea, first in a coaching capacity where his reputation as a player won him great respect. His skills as a communicator helped many a youngster.

And then, in July 1977 following the resignation of his old full-back partner Eddie McCreadie as manager, he was placed in charge.

Sadly, it just did not work out. There was a fair measure of ability on the staff. But there were gaps and weaknesses, too. And no money available to eliminate those shortcomings. So, after a wretched start to his second season, 1978–79, he was dismissed.

It was a sad end to a career during which he had served Chelsea FC long and faithfully.

Chelsea Career

123 appearances   2 goals

Peter Sillett – the penalty never to be forgotten

THE arrival of Peter Sillett at Chelsea was a direct result of his family's connections in Hampshire with Ted Drake, who had been born in Southampton, the club with which Sillett began his career.

Indeed, Sillett had been signed on at The Dell as a junior of 14 and ultimately graduated into the first-team, making 60 appearances in two seasons.

At the time of him coming to Chelsea he was still serving with the RAF and Southampton were loath to lose his services. But they were under financial pressure at the time and Peter was being courted by at least five First Division managers.

So, selling their most promising player was the Saints' reluctant solution.

In the early summer of 1953, a fee of £13,000 was agreed between the clubs and Drake persuaded Sillett's mother in a matter of five minutes, to let her son move to London.

He was immediately selected for the senior side at right-back, although he did not command a regular first-team place for the first 18 months or so, mainly due to the completion of his National Service and his consequent absence from full-time training.

Part of the deal with the Saints also included his younger brother, John, coming to Chelsea.

Once Peter had confirmed his place in the League side he was a fixture for the next six seasons.

Sturdily built - he turned the scales at 14st – he was a formidable opponent for wingers . Perhaps surprisingly for a man of his powerful build, he was not lacking in pace.

Three full England caps came his way, along with other appearances for England 'B' and Under-23 teams and the Football League representative XI.

Not the least of his qualities was his superb dead-ball kicking. Nearly all of his 34 goals, from 288 first-team games, came in this way. He was the regular penalty-kick taker throughout his time at the Bridge.

One such kick will always occupy a prominent place in the club's history. The occasion was the home game against Wolves, Chelsea's main challengers for the championship, in April 1954. With no score and time running out, the Wolves and England captain Billy Wright fisted a shot from Seamus O'Connell off the line.

Peter recalled it vividly. "Amongst the 75,000 crowd, I think the referee and me were the only two unsighted. Everyone else was going potty and after the lads had persuaded him to consult the linesman, he pointed to the spot.

"I had some 40 yards to walk up and everyone was shouting different comments and offering different advice. I remember their little winger, Johnny Hancocks, piping up, 'He'll stick in the net.' And I did."

Two weeks later the championship was won and the celebrations began.

Sadly a broken leg, before Sillett was 30, ended his League career prematurely. He played three seasons for Guildford City, earning more than he ever had done in the maximum-wage days with Chelsea, and then managed Ashford Town and, later, acted as chief scout with Hereford United for his brother, John.

"The best days of my time in football were with Chelsea. Great crowds and a wonderful atmosphere. When I was out injured I'd pull a cap over my eyes and go and stand among the fans to catch the humour."

Chelsea Career

288 appearances   34 goals

George Smith – a Chelsea record holder

IN the two decades leading up to the outbreak of World War Two the cheque book was rarely out of sight as expensive signings regularly arrived at Stamford Bridge in the club's effort to buy success. Only rarely, however, were large sums splashed out on defenders.

Thus, in the summer of 1921 the signing of a young Scottish full-back whose football career had been confined to playing in junior leagues north of the border aroused little interest.

His assignment was to take over the right-back position from Walter Bettridge, who had been a fixture in that defensive role for 12 seasons.

And such was the manager's confidence that he was pitchforked into the League side for the opening fixture of that season, even beginning his Stamford Bridge career on his supposedly weaker side by being played at left-back.

For the obligatory signing on fee of £10 he was to prove a wonderful investment. And by the time he retired more than ten years later, he had chalked up more first-team appearances than any other player had managed for Chelsea up to that time.

In the pre-season public trial game, manager Dave Calderhead, seeing him perform for the first time, and never a man given to extravagant opinion, agreed that 'Smith was in very good shape'.

Within a week he was playing in the senior side, against Blackburn Rovers at Ewood Park, partnered by the veteran, Jack Harrow, who already had 150 games under his belt.

George Smith was the ideal build for the role played by full-backs in those days. At 5ft 9in he tipped the scales at just over 11st, more than enough to cope with the lightweight wingers of the day.

Ready to provide cover to central defence when required, he rarely advanced beyond the halfway line as in those days wingers usually took up advanced positions. Indeed, never once in all his time did his name ever appear on the scoresheet.

Almost entirely he was concerned with shoring up a suspect defence in a generally unsuccessful side and, at the end of his third season in the team, he saw Chelsea relegated to the Second Division. While the next six campaigns were mostly successful, promotion was narrowly missed on several occasions until the spring of 1930. Then Smith dominated First Division wingers as if nothing had changed, even once transferring to his weaker side to accommodate the arrival of George Barber at right-back.

But time was against him and Tommy Law was still at the peak of his career. Past his 30th birthday, he returned north of the border to wind down his career with East Fife, leaving a Chelsea record of 370 senior appearances to stand for almost a quarter of a century.

Chelsea Career

370 appearances

Nigel Spackman – he always gave everything

AS a youngster Nigel Spackman always intended that football should be a pastime, a recreational activity, rather than a profession. In fact he was midway through a diploma course in business studies in his native Hampshire when a Bournemouth scout suggested he should go to Dean Court for trials. Successful though that proved, Spackman finished his college course first before committing himself.

Final exams successfully completed, he signed professional forms in May 1980, going on to make his first-team debut in Bournemouth's opening game, against York City at Bootham Crescent, three months later.

From that afternoon Spackman never looked back and was an automatic choice, going on to make 119 League appearances before his transfer to Chelsea in June 1983.

Thrilled at the opportunity, to make his mark on a bigger stage, he lost no time in proving himself.

His first season at Stamford Bridge was in Chelsea's promotion campaign of 1983–84. And his debut, in the opening game of that season, saw Spackman scoring in a 5-0 home victory over Derby County.

"It was great to see my first-ever shot for Chelsea go straight in. Fortunately I hit it well and it went through a mass of legs."

Not surprisingly, from that first day he had won the hearts of his new fans and, indeed, became one of the most popular players in a buoyant and successful team.

His attitude was first-class; his energy ceaseless. And he fitted easily into a 4–2–4 system. Whether defending or attacking, he was in his element.

And he was always mindful of his days at Bournemouth. "When you play in the lower divisions you have no illusions and it is an incentive to work at your game very hard to aim to reach the top. It is an excellent grounding."

Moving into the First Division was no problem and he played in every game in that first season, when Chelsea finished sixth in the championship table and reached the semi-final of the League Cup.

His workrate was non-stop. He would buzz about round opponents, closing them down, hustling and challenging before winning the ball. No one in his era at the Bridge could turn defence into attack more rapidly or to greater advantage

In his (too few) four seasons, if rarely spectacular and often taken or granted, there was no more influential or more reliable member of a consistently successful side.

It was certainly a shock to his fans when he left Chelsea in February 1987, and moved to Liverpool for a £400,000 fee.

However, it was a good move for Nigel, who won a League championship medal in 1987-88, and, for various reasons, necessary for Chelsea. But as Ken Bates summed up the feelings of so many, "He always gave everything for us on the field."

Chelsea Career

254-13 appearances   14 goals

David Speedie – Chelsea's angry wasp

THE 1982–83 season opened more in hope than expectation so far as Chelsea were concerned. A start had been made to renovate Stamford Bridge but money was in short supply and manager John Neal had made only two new signings of note.

One of these, David Speedie, for what turned out to be a bargain buy at £70,000 from Darlington, aroused little interest.

Only one victory had come from the first five Second Division fixtures when the Scot made his debut, against Oldham Athletic at the Bridge.

His effect on the forward line was instant. Buzzing around like an angry wasp, he scored both goals in Chelsea's 2-0 victory (and was narrowly denied a hat-trick) and then repeated the feat in the following home League game, against Grimsby Town.

The first goal moved Neal to describe it as 'the like of which I have never seen before, being a double-header setting himself up, and then finishing the move off which really demonstrated the lad has the right attitude'.

Twelve months later, the arrival of Kerry Dixon, from Reading, gave Chelsea possibly the most feared attacking duo in League football at that time.

Between them Speedie and Dixon scored 41 goals as Chelsea romped their way to promotion, with Speedie winning international recognition, first at Under-21 level, and then making his full debut against England at Hampden Park.

Few players down the years at Chelsea have shown greater commitment. His aggression did not always meet with the approval of referees, and opponents would often play on David's fiery temperament, sometimes to their own cost.

But, more importantly, his skills constantly shone through. His ball control would bring an awkwardly bouncing ball instantly down to his feet. For a small man (5ft 7in) his spring enabled him to outjump taller defenders and direct his headers powerfully past opposing goalkeepers. And then there was his pace and acceleration, not the least of his attributes.

In short, his presence was a constant menace to opponents, Or, as one writer so aptly put it, 'His various ingredients make him as difficult to stop as a handkerchief caught in a tornado.'

He had learned the hard way, so far as climbing the football ladder was concerned. Doncaster Rovers rejected him ('too small'). He then played for a Barnsley Sunday nursery team before Darlington gave him his first real chance.

Leaving Chelsea in July 1987, he joined Coventry City for a fee of £750,000 and spent four seasons at Highfield Road before moving to Liverpool in February 1991 (the last of Kenny Dalglish's signings), at the age of 31 still attracting a £675,000 fee.

And appearing for one more time at Stamford Bridge, with Liverpool, then mathematically in contention for the championship, Speedie, warmly greeted, scored a goal on his once-familiar stage, although it was Chelsea who upset the form book by winning 4-2. Speedie moved to Blackburn Rovers in August 1991.

Chelsea Career

197-8 appearances   64 goals

Dick Spence – Barnsley-born Cockney sparrow

DICK Spence was born in Barnsley and signed professional forms for his local club who introduced him to League football.

Watching him springing his way on foot down the Fulham Road to Stamford Bridge on match days, it was difficult to believe that he was reared in what had at one time been the most productive coal mining town in the world. Because in every way Dicky more resembled a Cockney sparrow.

He arrived in London in October 1934 and never left the capital, where he died at the age of 75 in 1983.

It is difficult to imagine him in any other profession and it was his ability as a schoolboy which sowed the seeds of an ambition to become a professional footballer.

Strangely he began his career as a centre-forward, but such a position was no place for a welterweight in the adult game played by miners on uneven surfaces among the pitheads. And so he soon switched to the open spaces on the wings.

Spence was one of manager Leslie Knighton's most successful acquisitions for Chelsea.

Immediately he made the transition to First Division football. When he arrived, eight League games had already gone but six months later he had been an ever-present and in his 34 appearances had scored no fewer than 19 goals – a Chelsea record for a winger which has never been exceeded. (Any comparison with Bobby Tambling is unfair since the latter was rarely regularly played in a similar role.)

His style and determination endeared him to spectators. Speed and acceleration were his strongest weapons. In those days full-backs were often heavily built and much less than mobile than in the present game.

Spence would tease and then by-pass them with his pace as if they were non-existent, often ending his raid on goal with a shot of tremendous and surprising power from such a lightweight.

Twice he wore an England shirt, against Austria and Belgium in 1936. But it was his misfortune to be a contemporary of Stanley Matthews.

Occasionally he would swap wings, especially after the arrival of the mercurial Peter Buchanan, but he was always happier on the right flank.

Having joined the Metropolitan Police at the outbreak of World War Two in 1939 (a curious recruitment for one of such small stature) he was mostly available for the seven seasons of regional football.

Then, in 1946, he was back at his normal post, spritely as ever at the age of 38 and now enjoying pin-pointing his crosses on to the head of Tommy Lawton.

It seemed as if he might go on for ever, but a broken leg ultimately ended his playing career, although not before he had chalked up another club record by being, at 39 years and 1 month, the oldest player to turn out for Chelsea in a Football League fixture.

But his Stamford Bridge days were by no means over (it was almost as if he had nowhere else to go!).

For nearly two more decades he worked on the training staff, travelling with both the 'A' team and Juniors.

The gaggle of spectators at their home games would eagerly await the opportunity for Dick to sprint on to the field, with dripping 'magic' sponge, to attend to injury and evoke memories of almost 40 years before.

And even after that he was still a Chelsea regular. Still light on his feet, he bounced along the Fulham Road, turning in through the Stamford Bridge gates as if guided by radar (presumably via his usual and long-standing bookmaker) to support the club that had been an integral part of his life.

Chelsea Career

246 appearances   65 goals

John Spencer – was his goal the best-ever?

THE signing of John Spencer from Glasgow Rangers in August 1992, for £450,000, was to prove an excellent investment for Chelsea.

Having already won international honours for Scotland at Youth and Under-21 level, he had found his progress at Rangers blocked by such as Ally McCoist and Mark Hateley, despite the fact that he was scoring 30 goals a season in the Reserves.

And at Chelsea, too, there was no easy passage into the first team with Mick Harford and Robert Fleck ahead of him in the queue.

A fixture on the substitutes bench to begin with, it was not until after his first Christmas at the Bridge that opportunity knocked. From then he never looked back, scoring seven times from 13 games in what was left of that season.

His original striking partners were Mark Stein or Paul Furlong and it was in Chelsea's first venture into European football for 23 years that he really made the headlines.

After the Czech team, Viktoria Zizkov, had been eliminated (4-2) in the first round of the UEFA Cup, came Austria Memphis (formerly known as Austria Vienna), and the home 0-0 draw clearly left Chelsea with a mountain to climb in the second leg. However, it was in this situation that John Spencer scored a truly memorable goal which lit up – and decided – the match.

Many present, indeed, claimed it was Chelsea's 'best-ever'.

In a desperate search to break the 0-0 stalemate, five minutes before half-time, and with Chelsea penned back in defence, Spencer was the first player to latch on to a rebound off Erland Johnsen, way back in defence,

With the Austrians somewhat off-guard, having pushed forward, little Spencer set off as high speed from inside his own half with the Memphis defenders in hot pursuit. His solo 70-yard sprint, crucially aided by Eddie Newton's decoy run, ended with the Scot easily rounding the goalkeeper and planting the ball into the net.

Dmitri Kharine later saved a penalty-kick and Chelsea hung on to their precious advantage and progressed into the next round on the away-goals rule.

Operating either in the centre or on the flanks of the attack, Spencer was rewarded with a regular place in Scotland's senior squad. Occasionally, not altogether to his liking, he would fill a midfield place.

In the 1995–96 season he was runner-up to Ruud Gullit in Chelsea's Player of the Year vote, when he mostly figured in a position behind the main strikers, a role which did not materially reduce his output of goals.

His manager would say that John Spencer was at his best when he was 'hungry' and perhaps that was why, like a caged lion, he was at times confined to the substitutes' bench.

Before he left Stamford Bridge, for Queen's Park Rangers, he confessed, "It gets harder every year; you have to add a wee bit extra to your game because defenders get to know your tricks."

John Spencer had four successful and eventful years at Chelsea and was one of the club's real characters, both on and off the field. Certainly the dressing-room was a quieter place after he had left.

His stay at Loftus Road was brief and he had a spell with Everton, before returning north of the border, to Motherwell.

Chelsea Career

100-37 appearances   43 goals

Willi Steffen – a legend after six months

CAN a player ever claim to be a club legend after a career of a mere six months.? Few who recall the immediate first post-World War Two season of 1946–47 would argue against the giant Swiss full-back, Willi Steffen, qualifying for such an accolade.

As normal football creaked back into action on 31 August 1946, Chelsea could call upon only one of their side which had opened the last normal season seven years earlier.

Admittedly, their shrewd manager Billy Birrell, had acquired a trio of experienced internationals at a considerable cost for those days, aiming to ensure the club's survival in the top division. A short-term measure. But there were ominous gaps, most particularly in defence, highlighted when Liverpool rattled seven goals into the Chelsea net at Anfield in the first away fixture of that season.

Not the least of the problems was the left-back position where the option lay between a 30-year-old survivor from the pre-war Combination team, still to make his senior debut, and a raw, untried, lad from Aylesbury whose experience was mainly confined to soccer in the Royal Navy.

Somehow Chelsea managed to keep clear of the First Division danger zone during the early weeks, hovering four of five places above the ultimate relegation places.

Then, on the last day of November, in their fixture against Derby County at the Baseball Ground, the name of Steffen appeared at left-back on the Rams' match programme, in a defensive barrier which was likely to be sorely tested by Derby's star-studded attack, as indeed was soon proved to be the case.

At least the programme managed the correct spelling of the newcomer's name (which was more than the Chelsea editor could manage a week later!). On a heavy, treacherous playing surface the Swiss international performed creditably and it was at once clear he had solved one of the club's more glaring weaknesses.

In fact he had already made an appearance at Stamford Bridge, which many had not realised, when he played for Switzerland against England the previous May in front of 75,000 spectators.

By the time his stay in England was up, five months later, he had made a further 19 appearances (missing only four games through injury), and had won the respect and affection of his fans.

Steffen had played six times altogether for his country. Superbly built and standing over 6ft tall, he was strong in the tackle and dominating in the air (an important asset in a defence lacking in this respect). Going forward with increasing acceleration, and with vocal encouragement from the terraces, he was a formidable sight for any opposition. But he was also the most stylish and artistic of players with clever footwork, and he never gave referees cause for concern.

Popular in the dressing-room – he had a penchant for practical jokes as well – it was a sad day when he made his last appearance for the club at the end of April.

He had certainly made the best possible use of his time in England. Apart from his great success on the field he returned home well-versed in the language, the sixth in which he could converse fluently.

A commissioned fighter pilot in the Swiss Air Force, he had been brought up in a small village outside Berne, the son of one of the largest fruit exporters in Switzerland.

Three weeks after bowing out of English League football he returned to Britain, playing for the Rest of Europe against Great Britain at Hampden Park in Glasgow, but thereafter was not seen here again.

Chelsea Career

15 appearances

Les Stubbs – provided beef among the lightweights

MOST of the Chelsea heroes who won the championship in 1954–55 (only 15 players made more than 10 appearances) have become household names, their places in the annals of the club's history assured.

Unfairly, one whose name too rarely figures is Leslie Stubbs, who was signed from Southend United for a £10,000 fee in November 1952 and returned to his only other League club six years later.

Indeed, he has lived all his life in Great Wakering, where he started with the local club and where he finished as a footballer, aged 52.

Manager Ted Drake had been impressed by the qualities of the sturdy Stubbs while managing Reading and he added strength to a lightweight forward line. Weighing 12st, he was not easily knocked off the ball; his height just under 6ft enabled him to be a force in the air.

"Yes, I think Mr Drake signed me to provide a bit of beef among the lightweights like Frankie Blunstone and little Eric Parsons," he said.

Stubbs scored only five goals in the championship year, although he stood down on several occasions to make way for the amateur Seamus O'Connell.

Probably the most crucial of all those goals was in the game against Wolverhampton Wanderers at Molineux at the beginning of December. At that time Wolves were in top place in the table with Chelsea starting to move into top gear but standing around halfway and not generally regarded as championship contenders.

With ten minutes of that game remaining Chelsea led 2-1, whereupon Wolves equalised and then went ahead as the result of a bitterly disputed penalty.

Previously both Stubbs and Parsons had had goals controversially disallowed, while a Roy Bentley effort which had appeared to cross the goal-line was also ignored.

Feelings were understandably running high and it was Les Stubbs who began the salvage operation. In front of the famous giant terrace at the town end of the Molineux ground, sandwiched between two defenders, he met a pass from Parsons to score a late equaliser.

And it was not too late for Roy Bentley to score a fourth, and winning goal, just before the final whistle. A goal, the significance of which became even greater four months later.

If not quite as crucial, probably the one Stubbs had scored seven days earlier was even more dramatic. At Stamford Bridge, against Portsmouth (also in contention at the top of the table), his enormous drive from some 40 yards range, and swept in on a gale, left the goalkeeper groping helplessly.

Centre-half, Ron Greenwood said afterwards, "Remember that one Les because you won't score many more like it."

So, if the big man's goal output that season may seem modest, he certainly twice hit the target when it really mattered.

For many years Stubbs never returned to the scene of his most influential footballing career but he became reacquainted with his former colleagues at a reunion some 40 years on. Still instantly recognisable, those years vanished and the reminiscences and chatter flowed.

"Chelsea was a wonderful experience. I earned a championship medal and a Charity Shield plaque and on summer tours they took me round the world."

Chelsea Career

123 appearances   35 goals

Bobby Tambling – the all-time goalscoring hero

BOBBY Tambling's all-time Chelsea goalscoring record has already stood for more than 30 years and, indeed, is certain to remain unchallenged in the forseeable future.

Impressive as that is, it is worth pointing out that his final tally of 202 first-team goals (from 370 competitive matches) was achieved before he reached the age of 30, when a persistent knee injury ended his Chelsea career all too early.

Tambling arrived at Stamford Bridge in 1957 to play for the juniors. A tally of 33 goals from 25 games (including seven hat-tricks) gave a hint of what was to follow and clearly his senior debut could not long be delayed

And so on 7 February 1959, manager Ted Drake produced Tambling (alongside another 17-year-old in Barry Bridges) in front of a 53,000 crowd for the game against West Ham United.

Fourteen minutes into that game Tambling had opened his scoring account. "My legs felt as if I haven't stopped running for 24 hours," he said afterwards.

One week later he failed to score; this time against Arsenal juniors on the Welsh Harp ground in Hendon.

Still used sparingly for the next two seasons, the departure of Jimmy Greaves accelerated his promotion to a regular place in the first-team, with Bridges his recognised striking partner.

Bobby was frequently regarded as Greaves' successor. And in a sense, he was. But they were totally different in both build and style. "It was no good trying to set myself up as another Greaves," Tambling said. "I had to pursue my own style."

This was based on fast running and acceleration which left defenders trailing and opened up a direct route to goal. His left foot was a powerful weapon and he could fire in shots on target without any slackening of pace.

Three times in a match he scored four goals, including once in a game now part of Chelsea's history.

On an evening in the second half of May 1963, Chelsea needed victory to clinch promotion after having spent one season in Division Two of the Football League.

As the ebullient manager Tommy Docherty, put it, "The boys go on the field knowing the ball is at their feet and the future is in their hands."

He had small need to worry. Bobby Tambling led the charge against opponents, Portsmouth, himself scoring his four goals in a 7-0 victory before leading his heroes into the directors' box in front of a 54,000 crowd, most of whom refused to disperse before they had fêted the team.

At Villa Park in September 1966, he went one better in scoring five times in Chelsea's 6-2 victory. The last of these goals was also his last kick of the game; removing a boot, he limped away down the tunnel, his job well and truly completed.

It is surprising that he won only three full international caps for England (he made 13 Under-23 appearances).

But it could all have been so different. The lad from Storrington in Sussex had taken time to adjust to the life of a professional footballer.

"After the first week as a groundstaff boy I was nearly in tears with homesickness. But I decided to keep it to myself and battle it out."

Chelsea Career

366-4 appearances   202 goals

Albert Thain – at home with trains rattling by

ALBERT Thain was one of Chelsea's 'foot soldiers'. Other have possessed more skills and achieved more in their chosen profession, but if perseverance and loyalty count for anything, the inside-forward from Southall, rates among the best.

His adult football career began with the Metropolitan Railway FC and, having caught the attention of League clubs after moving to the local club of his birthplace, Southall, he chose Chelsea.

"I knew I would settle there and feel at home" he jokingly explained. "Because I could listen to the underground trains rattling by!"

And settle down he certainly did. For nine happy years.

To begin with he found it difficult to adjust to his new life. But he persevered, responding to advice and full-time training, and for his first three seasons was a pillar in the Combination forward line.

In August 1925 he was given his first real chance in the senior side at inside-right, Andy Wilson moving across to the left to accommodate him. And for the next four seasons Albert Thain was a permanent fixture.

Previously there had been moments of doubt in his mind but he refused to be downhearted "I'll get there sooner or later," was his attitude and with that spirit he finally made it.

Indeed, supporters who regularly attended reserve games felt promotion to the seniors should have come earlier and when he did establish his place in the League team, his game improved markedly.

For his entire first-team career he was partnered by Jackie Crawford on the right wing, an excellent understanding between the two being one of the strengths of Chelsea in those days.

Albert had excellent ball-skills, while a deceptively long stride often carried him past larger, more heavily-built, defenders. For a man of relatively small frame, he possessed a powerful shot, as a total of 45 League and Cup goals in three seasons indicates.

And in those campaigns Chelsea, pressing for promotion from the Second Division, were never below fourth spot in the table.

At the age of 28, Thain could have expected his first-team career was only around the halfway mark after four most successful seasons.

But, sadly, injury struck and he was never the same player again. Although he returned to the Combination side and soldiered on for another two seasons, it became increasingly apparent that his days in the top flight were numbered and he moved down the ladder for a brief while with Bournemouth & Boscombe Athletic.

But Chelsea FC retained his affection. "I always felt very much at home there," he said later, "because even in the bath I could hear the trains going past."

And he continued to support Chelsea, even paying his own railway fare to watch his former colleagues in away games.

Chelsea Career

153 appearances   50 goals

Mickey Thomas – enthusiasm, industry, energy

MICKEY Thomas was a Chelsea player for less than two years – just one of his 13 clubs – yet in that short spell he established himself in the hearts of all the club's fans, with his undying enthusiasm for the cause as well as his wide range of individual skills.

Born in Mochdre, he was a true Welshman and with the love of football in his veins, although in later years he courted controversy off the field in more ways than one. It was while Thomas was awaiting a reply from Leeds United in 1970 that John Neal persuaded him to sign as an apprentice for Wrexham and an exciting and fruitful career was under way.

Having acquired four Welsh Youth caps, he graduated to full professional, made his League debut at 17, and remained at the Racecourse Ground for eight seasons, playing for his club in European competitions in three of them, and also picking up three Welsh Cup winners' medals and the first 11 of his full caps for his country.

Leaving Wrexham in 1978 to join Manchester United for £300,000 (a record fee for Wrexham), he then set out on a journey which was to see him playing for no fewer than ten different clubs before returning home to Wrexham 12 years later in 1991. There he had enjoyed some of the most memorable moments of his long career, including scoring a brilliant goal in the FA Cup against Arsenal in his club's 2-1 victory over the Football League champions.

It was John Neal again who signed him for Chelsea in, January 1984, Mickey making his debut against Derby County in a 2-1 victory at the Baseball Ground, and keeping his new club en route for promotion to the First Division, as champions.

Playing in every one of the remaining 17 League fixtures that season, he never looked back, captivating his new fans with enthusiasm, boundless energy and industry.

No-one ran throughout the 90 minutes of a game so apparently unceasingly, cajoling his team-mates to emulate his example. His indomitable fighting spirit was infectious.

At times his refusal to come out of any tackle, or situation, second-best brought him into conflict with opponents, or referees, but under the surface there was always lurking a sense of fun.

Who will ever forget his performance at Hillsborough, against Sheffield Wednesday in January 1985 in the second leg of a fifth-round Football League Cup-tie?

Indeed, John Neal summed it up as 'an extraordinary match... our brave players scoring four goals in the second half... to achieve a famous draw'. This after being three goals behind at half-time. The last-gasp fourth was scored by Mickey Thomas and was instrumental in gaining a replay, subsequently won by Chelsea, Thomas once more supplying the winner.

All this drama and excitement was crowded into Mickey's last days at the Bridge, before he moved to West Bromwich Albion the following September (for £100,000), clearly thought not to fit into the plans of new manager, John Hollins.

Albion was but one stop on his journey to another five clubs, before he ended his career back at Wrexham.

There was to be one further association with Chelsea. On 18 January 1986, Mickey lined up for West Brom – who were marooned at the foot of the First Division – against Chelsea at The Hawthorns, a game comfortably won 3-0 by the visitors.

The little man's every kick was cheered by visiting supporters (and several times acknowledged by the player himself).

"There's only one Mickey Thomas," was the hymn which rang up to the sky. And there certainly was! Albion fans listened in bewildered silence.

Chelsea Career

53 appearances   11 goals

Jack Townrow – he had his own ideas

THE careers of some footballers are comparatively uncomplicated. Others face challenges which require strength of character and the intelligence to adapt to changes as the game evolves.

One such was Jack Townrow, born in London and an engineer by trade. A commanding figure on and off the field, standing almost 6ft tall and weighing 13½st, he was ideally built for a central pillar around which a defence could be built.

An England Schoolboy player, his professional career began with Clapton Orient in August 1919, having been spotted while playing non-League football in East London with Fairbairn House.

As a centre-half he was one of those of his generation whose game was revolutionised by the introduction of the new offside law which was introduced in 1925.

Until then he had been noted for his versatility, then a hallmark of footballers occupying his position. Now up the field, now back again to defend.

Townrow, possessor of a shrewd football brain, had his own ideas about how deal with the new law.

He also achieved the not inconsiderable feat of catching the eyes of the England selectors while still playing for unfashionable Clapton Orient, and was selected against Scotland, at Hampden Park, and against Wales.

This alerted the Chelsea management and, aged 26, he moved to Stamford Bridge in February 1927 for the then considerable transfer fee of £5,000. Too late to aid the club's promotion drive, he was, however, the pillar around which the defence was built for the next four seasons.

Twice again, Chelsea narrowly failed to rejoin the top flight before promotion arrived in the spring of 1930.

At that time Townrow was at his peak and although never again attracting the attention of the England selectors, he was one of the outstanding defenders in the country.

Not that he was ever one prepared totally to conform to the role of the purely defensive pivot – an idea that was clearly not entirely to his liking. On occasions he simply could not resist adding his presence to the forward line. He never lost an opportunity to launch an attack, using an early ball with pin-point accuracy

He was also the complete centre-half; a sound positional sense, ana exceptionally strong and commanding in the air.

In the autumn of 1931, and now in his early 30s, his first-team days were ended by the signing of Peter O'Dowd, also an England centre-half. Townrow moved to Bristol Rovers where he wound down his playing career.

After leaving the playing side in 1932 he returned to tend the ground and coach Fairbairn House. He died, aged 68, in Knaresborough.

Chelsea Career

140 appearances   3 goals

Terry Venables – a vision few others possessed

IT was Jimmy Thompson, a prolific goalscorer for Chelsea in the late 1920s, whose gift for unearthing football talent in London's East End who was responsible for bringing Terry Venables to Stamford Bridge, with a host of other clubs in hot pursuit.

Venables arrived in 1958, a confident and independent-minded 15-year-old whose successful future in the game was never in doubt.

He timed his entry at the Bridge well. Manager Ted Drake was rebuilding a new team based on youngsters who quickly gave notice of their potential by winning the FA Youth Cup in the spring of 1958, with such as Ken Shellito, Barry Bridges and Jimmy Greaves in the line-up.

It was in February 1960 that Venables made his senior debut, in the away fixture against West Ham United (on his own doorstep as it were), before becoming a regular member of the first team the following season, taking the step up like a duck to water.

He was an outstanding midfield player, strong in the tackle and a brilliant passer of the ball with a tactical awareness which could turn defence into attack with a vision few others possessed. Drake was happy to let the young lad express himself.

Then in September 1961, Drake was replaced by Tommy Docherty. The Scot appeared to resent Venables' influence on the rest of the team. At the age of 19, Venables was captain of the side, a reflection of how he was regarded within the club. It was hoped that the new manager could work with him..

But that didn't happen. If things on the pitch were not unfolding to the original plan, the captain would change tactics to his own liking and without reference to the bench. It was a marriage destined never to survive. Then, of course, came the famous 'Blackpool Incident' when eight players were sent back to London by Docherty after vacating their hotel for a late-night drinking episode.

Next, in April 1966, after an FA Cup semi-final defeat for which, typically, Venables was in part held responsible, the player was transferred to Tottenham, having played his last game in a Fairs' Cup semi-final in Barcelona. An increasingly turbulent chapter had ended.

Seventeen months later, Tommy Docherty himself was dismissed by Chelsea, to be replaced by Dave Sexton and it is intriguing to speculate how Venables – and Chelsea – would have fared in such a partnership.

Terry was, of course, the complete midfield general with a wonderful sense of tactical awareness. His reading of the game and positional play were great strengths. Indeed, it was the hub around which Chelsea's football revolved for six seasons.

His constantly marshalled his fellow defenders and he demanded to be in the game for as much of the 90 minutes as was possible.

No one could translate a game from defence into attack more quickly than the 'Venner', which he regularly achieved with his accurate distribution.

Honours, of course, constantly came his way. He represented England at Schoolboy, Youth, Amateur, Under-23 and full international levels. He was in Spurs' FA Cup-winning team against Chelsea in May 1967, having played in Chelsea's League Cup winning sides against Leicester City in 1965.

As a manager he took Crystal Palace from the Third Division into the First and later won the Spanish League championship with Barcelona, before returning to take over a succession of clubs in this country, including Spurs and Leeds United, briefly. He managed England from 1994 to 1996, although his career has been marred by bad publicity over his business dealings, a factor which caused him to leave the England job.

Chelsea Career

237 appearances   31 goals

Gianluca Vialli – the fans just couldn't believe it

NEVER before in the history of Chelsea Football Club had the arrival of a player created so much interest. Indeed, Gianluca Vialli's signing on a free transfer in May 1996 was greeted with almost disbelief by the fans.

Aged 32, he had already won a catalogue of honours in his club career with Cremonese, Sampdoria and Juventus: the Italian championship (twice); four Italian FA Cups; the European Cup-winners' Cup; Italian Super Cup (twice); UEFA Cup winner. And he had also captained Juventus to the Europeans Champions Cup in 1996.

By comparison, 59 international caps for his country (and 16 goals) seemed almost to pale beside these club trophies.

Yet Vialli, was brimming with enthusiasm and prepared for his new challenge, well aware that past reputation would count for little, if anything.

First, he had to master a new language ("I need to talk to my teammates about football, but also about life"); then he had to find a permanent home after first living in hotels.

Above all, he was anxious to get to know his new colleagues: "I like them... they are very funny... they always joke... but when the match starts they become professional".

Not for one moment did he have any doubts that he had made the right move, even though he found pre-season training especially hard and he had to contend with a stubborn calf injury at the same time.

After a slow start to the 1996–97 season, Chelsea, if never in serious contention for the Premiership title, retained a position comfortably in the top half of the table and won their way to the FA Cup Final, where Middlesbrough were beaten in a drab game.

But all was not plain sailing for Gianluca. He had fitness problems from the beginning, and after scoring 10 goals from 16 starts, he lost his automatic first-team place to the striking duo of Mark Hughes and Giafranco Zola, often frustratingly watching from the substitutes' bench. He was in that position for the FA Cup Final itself before being summoned on to the field for the final two minutes – to a riotous reception.

Months before, however, Vialli had, along with Zola and Mark Hughes, played a memorable role in steering Chelsea towards that Final, in a 4-2, fourth-round, victory over Liverpool at Stamford Bridge. Chelsea came back from two goals down at half-time, Vialli scoring the last two goals which clinched a famous victory, the last a powerful header crowning a darting run. It is a game permanently etched in CFC history.

However, after three seasons when he missed almost one third of the fixtures mainly through injury, time was running short for the great man and in August 1999 he announced that he had retired as a player 'unless emergencies dictate', and he never appeared in the first team again.

But already his 'second' Chelsea career was under way. Early in February 1998, Ruud Gullit was dismissed as manager of Chelsea and was immediately replaced by Vialli after what the new incumbent understandably described as 'one of the most amazing weeks in Chelsea's history'.

At the time the club occupied third place in the Premiership table, and were en route to winning both the European Cup-winners' Cup and the Football League Cup.

It was scarcely a situation normally leading to a managerial dismissal. But there were internal personal difficulties involving Ruud Gullit.

Then, having steered Chelsea to their second FA Cup Final victory in three years, Vialli himself was dismissed early in 2000–01, when it seemed that the team apparently was not moving forward as expected.

Maybe it was a harsh decision but one which was eventually justified by the passage of time.

Be that as it may, Gianluca Vialli, will always occupy a special place in Chelsea's history. He brought success and passion to Stamford Bridge, and was liked and greatly respected by his players and army of spectators.

As a player, injury problems perpetually dogged his days, although his 40 goals from 69 starts would have been more than acceptable to most footballing mortals. He later managed Watford.

When he walked into the club he announced, "I want to be a legend at Chelsea – and that he certainly is."

Chelsea Career

69-19 appearances   40 goals

Tommy Walker – rich entertainment wherever he played

IT was a most auspicious afternoon in the late summer of 1944 when Sergeant Tommy Walker, serving in the Army with the Royal Corps of Signals, strode into Stamford Bridge to make his debut as a guest player for Chelsea against Fulham.

Not that the afternoon had a happy ending, with the Craven Cottage side winning 7-4, despite Walker scoring twice.

For the next few weeks he continued in his number-8 blue shirt, playing five games with seven more goals further emphasising his pedigree.

Whether or not that brief taste of English football influenced his decision to join Chelsea on a permanent basis is difficult to say, but in September 1946 manager Billy Birrell, signed his fellow countryman for a bargain £6,000.

No player in the club's history could have made a more instant impression, Walker, a Scottish international, scoring two goals on his home debut against Leeds United. And along with fellow internationals, Tommy Lawton and Len Goulden, he provided rich entertainment whenever he played.

His ball control was immaculate; his mazy dribbles left defenders wrong-footed and trailing in his wake. For a man past the age of 30, his acceleration was amazing and his distribution, with accurate passes invariably reaching colleague on the far wing, provided countless goalscoring opportunities.

In his 27 months at Stamford Bridge he scored 24 goals in just over 100 games for Chelsea.

All this, of course, added to his already established international reputation (21 caps for Scotland when such fixtures were less in number than today). It was playing for his country against England in 1936 that he scored a goal which is still recalled.

Scotland were awarded a penalty but the wind was so strong that the ball had to be placed on the spot three times before the kick could be taken. Finally, Walker hurried into action, lest the wind shifted it again, and coolly blasted the ball past the England goalkeeper to earn a 1-1 draw. Other goals which also lived in memory were a couple of rockets from 40 yards' range in Scotland's 4-2 victory against Wales in 1939.

Before he left Chelsea, he had made his mark off the field too. He was closely involved in church and youth club work in South London as well an constantly accepting invitations to assist charities.

His final game for Chelsea was on Boxing Day 1948, at Fratton Park, Portsmouth. Both teams formed up in line to applaud Tommy Walker from the pitch at the end of the game, with Pompey's president, Field Marshall Viscount Montgomery of Alamein, standing to attention as he disappeared from view.

And so back to Edinburgh where he later managed his beloved Heart of Midlothian (for whom he had played between 1932 and 1946), to win two Scottish League championships before being awarded the OBE for services to football. He later managed Dunfermline and Raith Rovers.

Tommy Walker died in hospital in January 1993, a few days after being spotted by a close friend assisting an elderly woman off a bus. A perfect gentleman on and off the field.

Chelsea Career

104 appearances   24 goals

Sammy Weaver – progressive and polished

DERBYSHIRE-BORN, Sammy Weaver nevertheless made his name on Tyneside, first appearing for Newcastle United at the age of 20.

'Progressive and polished' was one description of his game. And he was, of course, the first to introduce the 'long throw' practised anywhere from the edge of the opposition penalty area to the corner flag. 'As good as a corner kick,' it was said and certainly it was the longest throw seen in football up to that time.

He began in the game playing for local clubs, and in particular, Sutton United.

Hull City was his first League club, in March 1928. But that was always going to be merely a stepping stone to higher things and Newcastle snapped him up in November 1929.

At once the Geordies took him to their hearts and it is no exaggeration to say that he was a major driving force in steering his new club into the 1932 FA Cup Final against Arsenal, which United won 2-0.

Weaver made the game look easy, as indeed it was for him. He was a dominant figure in midfield with his long, easy, stride. His distribution was invariably inch-perfect and it is surprising that he won a mere three international caps, all of them prior to arriving at Stamford Bridge.

In the spring of 1934, Newcastle United were relegated and the fact that the club was unable immediately to return to what they considered their rightful place in the top class of the Football League was undoubtedly the reason for Weaver's move to Stamford Bridge.

Here he succeeded the long-serving 'Dusty' Miller at left-half which Miller had occupied virtually unchallenged for the previous 12 seasons.

The regrettable thing about Weaver's Stamford Bridge days was that they were so short, terminated as they were by the start of World War Two.

Maybe some of the dynamite had gone from his game when he came to Chelsea. But, assuming the captaincy 12 months after his arrival, he was nevertheless still a star performer.

The ideal foil to the aggressive terrier-like Irish international, Billy Mitchell, on the other flank of midfield, Weaver's constructive use of the ball ensured a generous service to the forward line.

As one of those who benefited from his artistic skills once said, "Never have I received a more accurate, or more thoughtful service."

Weaver's three seasons at the Bridge brought typically mixed, and unpredictable, results. Very much in Chelsea's inter-war style. Finishes of 13th and 10th respectively in Sammy's first two years were followed by the narrowest of escapes (20th place) in May 1939.

But that season, again in typical fashion, Chelsea saved their best for the big occasions. Arsenal were beaten on two occasions at Stamford Bridge, 4-2 and, in the FA Cup, 2-1. Fulham and Sheffield Wednesday were also dismissed in the same competition before the Pensioners made an unexpected and somewhat undignified exit in the sixth round against Grimsby Town at the Bridge.

For three wartime seasons Weaver continued to turn out for Chelsea, making his final appearance in October 1942. His League career ended with two games for Stockport County in 1946.

He was also a useful cricketer, playing two matches for Somerset in the County Championship in 1939, and was later masseur to Derbyshire.

Almost his last appearance on a football field was at The Den in the 1950s. A Millwall player required treatment and, sponge dripping, the trainer sprinted across. "He runs as if he had been a footballer in his time," someone said.

An accurate observation. Indeed it was Sammy Weaver, almost 50 and still serving the game he had adorned so stylishly.

Chelsea Career

125 appearances   4 goals

David Webb – brave, determined, larger than life

OF all the Chelsea goals – now in excess of 6,000 – scored down the years, it is safe to say that David Webb's header, 14 minutes into extra-time in the 1970 FA Cup Final replay against Leeds United at Old Trafford, must surely rate as one of the most important, and certainly the most frequently recalled.

"Ian Hutchinson's long throw clipped the top of Jack Charlton's head and flew across the crowded goalmouth and I knew it was neck or nothing as I climbed above two opponents to get to the ball. It wasn't a proper header at all. The ball caught me just above the left eye, but all that mattered was that it went in!"

Yet 18 days earlier, in the first game at Wembley, Webb's experience had been somewhat different as Leeds' winger Eddie Gray had given him an embarrassing time with his pace and skill on the ball, although the defender redeemed himself by blocking a last-minute shot on the goal-line, which allowed Chelsea to fight another day.

David Webb played almost another 300 games for Chelsea, one of them in an emergency wearing the goalkeeper's jersey and triumphantly keeping a clean sheet.

An East Ender, he started his career on Orient's groundstaff where he played under the control of Dave Sexton, before moving to Southampton in March 1966, playing 75 games in two years with the Hampshire club.

From the start he was always one to catch the eye, both for his spectacular deeds on the field as well as for his constantly changing hair styles.

His game was founded on bravery, determination and strength of character. Others may have boasted greater natural ability, but none could better his appetite and desire. He was equally at home in the centre of defence or at full-back. Or even, in an emergency at centre-forward. Playing as a striker in two consecutive games in the 1971–72, he responded typically by scoring four goals.

For almost seven seasons he was a fundamental piece in the Chelsea jigsaw. Unhappily, he left Stamford Bridge before his 30th birthday when, for various reasons, the 1970 FA Cup-winning side began to fall apart.

"It upset me when the team was broken up to pay for that big lump of concrete [the East Stand]. Perhaps if the present chairman had been at Chelsea, then some way would have been found to keep the side together and solve the financial problems. But I've still got my medals in a box and wouldn't part with them for anything. And I spent six and a half wonderful years at the Bridge and that was the longest I was with any club."

Even so, Webby left without having a testimonial, moving on to play for Leicester City, Derby County and Bournemouth.

Almost 19 years later, in March 1993, he returned as manager after 11 games had passed without victory. After a 1-0 win in his first home game in charge, he ensured Chelsea would survive in the First Division, but his position was not confirmed at the end of the season and Glenn Hoddle was appointed.

Webb had further spells as manager, with Bournemouth, Torquay United and Southend United (twice), winning promotion in each of his two spells with the Essex club, as well as turning out for the reserve team at the age of 44.

He was certainly a larger-than-life character and never one to shirk a challenge.

Chelsea Career

299 appearances   33 goals

Bob Whittingham – a giant of a goalscorer

PROBABLY not until Jimmy Floyd Hasselbaink arrived at Chelsea at the beginning of the 2000–01 season was Bob Whittingham's reputation as having possessed the most powerful shot in the club's history challenged.

Both opponents, and his own colleagues, were in awe of the bullets fired, mainly from his stronger right foot, often at the most unexpected times from seemingly impossible positions and narrow angles.

He did not always find the target, of course, but his 34 goals in his first full season of 1910–11 was a club record which stood for 50 years.

Strong as an ox, although he stood only around 5ft 8in, he tipped the scales at a fraction under 13st. Square-shouldered, Whittingham seemed to remove opponents from his path as if they were not there. In fact, almost certainly they were relieved to have avoided physical contact.

A tale of those days before World War One told of an opposition full-back angrily criticising his goalkeeper for failing to prevent a goal from one of Whittingham's long-range rockets. The full-back accused him of a half-hearted effort.

"Why didn't you stop that one?" he stormed; to which the goalkeeper replied, "What's the bloody net for?"

Chelsea, trying to avoid relegation, made five late signings, including Whittingham from Bradford City. It was this flurry of action some three weeks from the end of the 1909–10 campaign which caused the League to introduce the law banning all transfer deals from the middle of March for the rest of the season.

However, even Bob Whittingham failed to prevent what had seemed probable for several weeks. On the final day, against Tottenham Hotspur, Chelsea controlled the play for much of the afternoon but lost 2-1 and down the club went, thanks to a goal from Percy Humphreys, who had moved from Stamford Bridge to White Hart Lane a few weeks earlier.

Whittingham seemed destined to be on stage for such end-of-season dramas. At Bradford City he had been in the team which escaped relegation by winning their final fixture of the season.

And after the relegation drama in 1910, 12 months later, his 30 League goals were not enough to erase that memory at Tottenham. With Chelsea needing to win at Gainsborough Trinity on the last day of the season to ensure promotion, Whittingham was unable to add to his club record total. Chelsea were defeated 3-1 and finished third.

However, promotion was achieved 12 months later, Whittingham scoring 26 goals (18 more than his nearest rival) and he went on to spend his final four seasons at Chelsea in the top flight.

Although he had failed to hit the net in the last game, against Bradford who were beaten 1-0, he was very much the hero of the hour, appearing to take his curtain call at the end of the match wearing nothing but a huge towel and a happy smile.

During the five wartime seasons, Whittingham played for his 'home' club, Stoke, and having played for England against Scotland in a Victory international, was transferred to the Potters in September 1919, thus ending his highly successful, and most eventful, Chelsea career.

Soon afterwards, the mighty-framed sharp shooter became ill and, sadly, died before the age of 40.

Chelsea Career

129 appearances   80 goals

Stan Wicks – he made the job so simple

EVERY football club has it tragedies and, its setbacks. And one name, sadly too often forgotten, which occupies a proud place in Chelsea's history is that of Stanley Maurice Wicks.

After putting together his team to win the Football League championship in 1954–55, when questioned as to his best bargain buy, Ted Drake hesitated between Wicks and Frank Blunstone.

"They were both bargains. Tremendous players too. And it was a tragedy that both their careers were cut short by injury. Of course, we saw Stan emerging as a superb defender. He was a terrific fellow, and he would have become England's centre-half forever and a day, like Jack Charlton did later on."

Drake had first signed Wicks soon after he took up his only previous managerial post, at Reading. And the youngster, just turned 20, went on to play 161 League games before Drake again secured his services, taking him away from the town of his birth where he had graduated into senior football. This time Drake roused the giant from his bed on a frosty, moonlit night to sign on the dotted line.

Ted knew what he wanted. By then his centre-half at Chelsea was the legendary Ron Greenwood, now past the age of 30 and in his second spell at Stamford Bridge where he had first arrived as a junior in pre-war days.

The stylish and unflappable Greenwood kept the young pretender at bay for almost a year, but once Wicks was given his opportunity in the first team there was no turning back.

His Chelsea career began at Christmas. On the morning of 25 December, Chelsea lost a vital League fixture at Highbury, 1-0, Tommy Lawton touching in the winner for the Gunners. It signalled the end of Greenwood's second Stamford Bridge chapter.

Twenty-four hours later, in the return match at the Bridge, Wicks was selected to mark Lawton and hardly gave the great man a kick. Not surprisingly, he retained his place, not missing a single one of the remaining fixtures,. He grew in stature as the weeks went by and, of course, qualified for his championship medal.

For one more complete season Wicks played in every game, holding together a side that was gradually disintegrating through age. Chelsea sank to 16th place in the table and it was clear that a massive rebuilding programme was required; one in which Wicks would have been a pivotal figure.

But it was not to be. On 19 September 1956, on a pleasant early autumn evening, and with speculation on Wicks becoming an England player, the blow fell.

Defending the railway end of Stamford Bridge, against Sheffield Wednesday, he damaged his knee ligaments so badly that he never played football again. He had made a mere 81 appearances for the Pensioners, as they were known in those days, scoring one goal.

Not only was he a highly skilled and creative player, he was scrupulously fair, and possessed an elegant and unhurried style. He was greatly respected by opponents and immensely popular with the fans.

As Chelsea's goalkeeper Chic Thomson, said, "Stan makes my job simple. He gets every ball in the air and doesn't miss many tricks on the ground."

Most sadly of all, Stan Wicks died on 20 February 1983, at the early age of 54.

Chelsea Career

81 appearances   1 goals

Harry Wilding – utterly dependable, ever willing

STANDING over 6ft tall and turning the scales at almost 13st, Harry Wilding was an imposing figure both on and off the field.

Born in Wolverhampton, he joined Chelsea in April 1914 but before he could play for the club, World War One had started and Wilding had been posted overseas to serve his country in the Army.

Indeed, not until August 1919 did he make his debut for the club when, playing at centre-forward, he had the distinction of scoring the first official League goal for Chelsea in four years.

By then, though, another and more permanent distinction had come his way with the award of the Military Medal.

Wilding had played for no other club before arriving at Stamford Bridge and was 24 when his professional football career began. Lacking experience, he was very much thrown in at the deep end. But he never looked back.

Tutored by Bob Whittingham and Jimmy Croal and, soon after by Jack Cock, he fitted easily into his new profession.

But centre-forwards are expected to score goals and Wilding could not produce in this respect, so he was quickly moved to inside-forward alongside Cock, another holder of the Military Medal.

Wilding never became a distinguished footballer quite in the top drawer. But he was utterly dependable and an ever-willing horse. Repeatedly it was said of him, 'He never plays a bad game'.

Versatility was a strong point. After half a dozen games as a forward he was switched to centre-half, for which position his build was ideally suited. Then he was tried at both wing-half positions – all in his first season.

After that it was in the centre of the defence that he really settled, and gave sterling service. Yet he was always ready to fill a gap elsewhere, in the half-back line or in the forward line. He was a model professional.

A man with a sense of humour, too. He never scored more than four League goals in a season, nor did he play in more than 40 League games. But then, with a smile on his face, he would say that the Guards never taught him to count beyond four. Or was it 40?

During his years at the Bridge he had mixed experiences. Defeat in the 1920 FA Cup semi-final against Aston Villa in Sheffield was a big disappointment and, even more depressingly, relegation to Division Two in April 1924.

He was very much a central figure in the final fixture of that season, against Manchester City at Stamford Bridge.

Needing to win on that afternoon by a considerable margin, hopes were raised when Chelsea scored three times in the first quarter of an hour, Wilding having been moved from defence into the forward line to boost the attack. And, indeed, he did score two of those goals. But the momentum could not be sustained, Chelsea won 3-1, but it proved insufficient. And Wilding never again played in the First Division.

Another game still occasionally recalled was a sixth-round FA Cup-tie against Cardiff in 1927. A goalless draw at Stamford Bridge was followed by a 3-2 defeat in the replay at Ninian Park. And poor Wilding was, most unfortunately, the villain.

At 2-2, the game was still wide open when an awkwardly bouncing ball touched his hand, quite accidentally. But a penalty was nevertheless awarded, from which Cardiff scored and went on to win the Final and take the trophy out of England for the only time.

At the age of 34, the big man moved to Tottenham Hotspur, and played a dozen first-team games before finally winding down his career with Bristol Rovers.

Chelsea Career

265 appearances   25 goals

Ray Wilkins – jewel from the youth scheme

CHELSEA were one of the first clubs to realise the importance of by-passing the high-priced transfer market by inaugurating their own youth scheme. It was in 1947 that their juniors began to compete in organised leagues under the name Tudor Rose.

The results, measured in terms of producing players to graduate to senior football, were disappointing. However, in the autumn of 1973 there emerged a priceless jewel by the name of Raymond Colin Wilkins, who followed his elder brother, Graham, into the professional ranks.

Promotion was swift and on 27 October that year, Ray Wilkins made his first-team debut at Stamford Bridge against Norwich City, coming off the substitutes' bench to replace David Webb.

They were difficult days at Stamford Bridge. The 1970 and 1971 Cup-winning team had fallen apart. The club was in financial crisis and clearly the ship was foundering. It was hardly the ideal situation for a teenager to break into senior football. Or, indeed, to take the place of the hugely talented Alan Hudson.

Yet, undeterred by the political shenanigans developing off the field 'Butch' set to work by example, his wonderful skills rising above the mediocrity of those around him, and tutored and encouraged by a new manager, Eddie McCreadie, whose drive and encouragement was one of the more positive factors at the time.

Even so, and inevitably, relegation became a reality in the spring of 1975 with Ray now Chelsea's youngest-ever captain.

Soon, however, he had caught the England manager's eye, ultimately becoming Chelsea's most-capped player, (up to that time) and leading his club to promotion in May 1977 after two seasons in the Second Division.

No one could have worked harder, or more willingly, for the cause. Operating mainly in front of the back-four defensive wall, his passing was immaculate, both in its range and accuracy. It was said that sometimes he lacked ambition - content to play 'safe' balls rather than going for the pass which would split open the opposition defences.

Later in his career, with Manchester United and in both Italian and French football, his range and vision had noticeably increased its scope.

He was also a fine marksman and was the club's leading scorer in 1975–76.

Sadly, for Chelsea, he moved to Manchester United in August 1979, aged 23, for a then, club record fee of £875,000, both to alleviate the mounting financial crisis at Stamford Bridge and also to further his own career.

By now he had become recognised as one of the country's leading midfield players, and moved to AC Milan in June 1984, and Paris St Germain three years later.

In November 1989, after two months with Glasgow Rangers, Wilkins returned to London still an influential and consistent player at the age of 33 and was player-manager at QPR and also played for Hibs. It was a matter of regret that he chose Queen's Park Rangers rather than Chelsea to end his career in England.

Nevertheless he remains one of Chelsea's greats.

Chelsea Career

193-5 appearances   34 goals

Stan Willemse – enjoyed every minute

FOREVER associated with Chelsea's 1954–55 championship heroes, Stan Willemse had already been at Stamford Bridge for five years, arriving from Brighton & Hove Albion in July 1949 for a £7,500 bargain fee.

Manager Billy Birrell had signed him to replace the Welsh international, cultured left-back Billy Hughes, already in his 30th year. But, within a month, Willemse had made his first-team debut in the testing atmosphere of Highbury Stadium, where Chelsea defeated Arsenal, 3-2.

He was a rugged, totally fearless defender who, almost certainly in the modern era, would have become a familiar name in referees' notebooks. In fact, 'the Tank', as he was known, was never sent-off and collected only one booking in 220 first-team games.

On the opposite flank for most of the latter part of that 1954-55 season, Peter Sillett presented a contrast to Willemse's lion-hearted up-and-at-'em approach. There were no frills to the newcomer's game. But he was an inspiration to his colleagues, and a formidable foe to opponents. A real 90-minute competitor.

During his Stamford Bridge career he won honours at both England 'B' level, and with the Football League XI.

In those days it was, of course, tactically a different game. Willemse's job was to dominate his opposing outside-rights. And they were certainly a rich vintage with such as Tom Finney of Preston, Jimmy Delaney (Manchester United and Scotland) and Peter Harris (Portsmouth in their two championship seasons.)

But top of Stan's list, and not surprisingly, was Blackpool's Stanley Matthews.

"He hated being tight-marked," Stan recalls. "He wanted plenty of space, but I think I played him as well as anyone.

"In some ways Finney caused more problems. He was so clever in drawing you out of position and giving you the slip."

On isolated occasions Willemse would be drafted into the forward line, at outside-left, and was by no means out of his depth. Indeed, in a vital fixture against Sunderland in Chelsea's run-in to the championship in March 1955, he scored a crucial goal in the 2-1 win.

Still supremely fit at the age of 32, he was transferred to Leyton Orient, for a £4,500 fee, and played for them for two seasons before retiring to Brighton, where he was born.

Indeed, for much of his time at the Bridge he would travel up daily on the *Brighton Belle* train along with John McNichol and Eric Parsons.

"I enjoyed every minute of my time in football," Stan reminisced after retiring. By today's standards the money was far from good – £20 a week, plus £2 bonus for a win and £1 for a draw. But, for winning the championship, we each got a new suit, an overcoat, and a trip to Paris. And, of course, that precious medal."

Apart from his defensive duties, he was also Frank Blunstone's 'minder'. When the little winger was attracting rough treatment, Stan would verbally issue his own version of a yellow card to the opponent. And that would be the end of the problem

Yes, indeed, different times. On occasions, after a match Stan would even share a bath with the referee and have a chat.

And he said not long ago, "Today I don't think I would even have got on the pitch without being booked!"

Chelsea Career

221 appearances   2 goals

Andy Wilson – always recognised, always fêted

ANDY Wilson was a dominant figure at Stamford Bridge for more than eight seasons, arriving as successor to Jack Cock at centre-forward in November 1923 for a £6,500 fee, a considerable sum in those days. Even after his retirement as a player he continued to live in London and was a regular spectator at Stamford Bridge into the 1970s. And he was always recognised and always fêted .

His first task which he set himself at Stamford Bridge was to keep Chelsea in the First Division. This he did not manage to do and, in fact, it was six years before he captained the team to promotion.

Football was always going to be his life. When asked when he began to learn the game, he replied, "Only a wee while before I learned to walk."

His service at Chelsea spanned nine seasons during which he played 253 first-team games and scored 62 goals.

While at Dunfermline Athletic, after the end of World War One, he was appointed captain and undoubtedly it focussed his mind and taught him to study the game more closely than he might otherwise have done.

His subsequent transfer to Middlesbrough equally advanced his football education, especially in the differences of the game south of the border.

He was one of the game's 'thinkers'. Not long after he arrived at Stamford Bridge an alteration was made to the offside law, resulting in effects never envisaged by the authorities.

Not the least important result was almost the universal adoption of the 'W' formation and Wilson, then recognised as an orthodox centre-forward, moved to an inside-forward position.

Here, as one of the 'feet' in the 'W', he became a true artist rather than the workhorse of previous days. With the ball at his toes he would lure opponents towards him, deceiving them by pushing the ball to a nearby colleague, or switching the point of attack with a long ball out to the opposite wing.

It was almost as if he was engaging in a game of chess. Even so, in this new role he remained a consistent goalscorer although such as Bob Turnbull (53 goals in two seasons) and, later, Hughie Gallacher and George Mills were other beneficiaries.

Having guided Chelsea back into the First Division he maintained his position for another two seasons before dropping out at the age of 34, in the autumn of 1931.

Briefly he played for Queen's Park Rangers and then, also for a short time in France, before managing Walsall for three seasons in the mid-1930s.

He became a good golfer, with a single-figure handicap, was an expert billiards player and picked up more trophies on the bowling green than he had ever won on the football pitch.

However, life had presented its problems to Andy Wilson. World War One had left him with a near-useless left arm. Also, through the latter days of his life as a player, he had a tendency to put on weight; even during his early years in the game he had weighed 12½st, although he stood only 5ft 6½in tall.

Born in Lanarkshire, he was a converted Londoner and continued to live within walking distance of Stamford Bridge, taking up his reserved seat in the centre block of the old East Stand, to a constant buzz of excitement, almost to the end of his life.

His son, Jimmy, joined the Chelsea professional staff in 1950, but alas never followed his father's footsteps into the first team.

Chelsea Career

253 appearances   62 goals

Jimmy Windridge – the Chelsea Wizard

THE 'Chelsea Wizard', as he was christened by the Stamford Bridge fans in the club's first season of 1905–06, was one of the earliest of all the signings in the team hastily assembled after the club's unexpected election to the Football League that April.

Jimmy Windridge was born and bred in the Birmingham district of Sparkbrook and began his career with Second Division club Small Heath (later Birmingham City), playing for them in one of the local leagues. Elevated into the Football League by Chelsea, at a cost of £190, he was to prove a wonderful investment.

He was at inside-left in the club's first-ever fixture, at Stockport, on 2 September 1905, and for the next five seasons he was absent only through injury.

Jimmy was a member of the promotion team in 1906-07, and less happily, still a regular in the side when relegation came in April 1910.

The fans loved him, both for his skills on the ball, and for his indomitable spirit. In many ways he was a typical product of his era. Quite simply his task was to unlock opponents' defences, which he regularly achieved with his complete mastery of the ball and intricate footwork.

George Hilsdon, in particular, owed Windridge's skill for many of his goals, laid on with precision either on the ground, or in the air.

But, he was certainly not only a creator of chances for others. Over 50 goals scored himself, at an average of more than one for every three games played, is a more than respectable output for an 'old-fashioned' winger.

Not surprisingly he won eight international caps for England spread over two years (1908–09), playing against such opposition as Austria (twice) Hungary and Bohemia.

Nearing the age of 30, his form began to dip, and with the arrival of Vivian Woodward and the other signings of new forwards, he was called upon less regularly.

In fact, it turned out to be much in Windridge's interests for, moving to Middlesbrough, far from winding down, his career again took off and he held his place in their First Division team for three seasons, before returning to Birmingham in 1914, where he scored 19 goals in 61 League and Cup games before retiring during World War One.

Twice more he came back to Stamford Bridge, wearing the unfamiliar red shirt of his new employers. On the first occasion he may have had mixed feelings as 'Boro returned to Teesside with a 3-2 victory under their belts. Jimmy starred on his familiar territory once more, not surprisingly. Or as the *Official Programme* said, 'He knows his way around the place.'

A batsman and medium-pace bowler, he played cricket for Warwickshire, too, making seven appearances (he once kept the legendary Yorkshire bowlers George Hirst and Wilfred Rhodes at bay for some time until he ran out of partners).

He lived in Birmingham until his death in September 1939.

Chelsea Career

152 appearances   58 goals

Dennis Wise – adding a buzz around the Bridge

THE arrival of Dennis Wise at Chelsea from Wimbledon, for a sum of £1.6 million, raised a few eyebrows; it was a Chelsea club record fee at that time – £100,000 more than the money paid for Andy Townsend the other major newcomer.

Manager Bobby Campbell, probably more prophetically than he realised, said that Wise would 'add a buzz around Stamford Bridge'.

Initially Chelsea fans did not know what to expect and many were somewhat sceptical.

Fortunately, his debut, against Derby County at Stamford Bridge, went well. Immediately he began to jink his way though the opposition and was voted man of the match ahead of Chelsea's hero of those days, Kerry Dixon.

Wise was happy. "It's nice to be liked by the crowd – it's a great feeling." And realistically he added, "I think the side could mature into one challenging and winning titles."

Already, of course, he had made his name with Wimbledon, not least in the 1988 FA Cup Final, and had come a long way from his days as a junior at Southampton where his potential was overlooked. And he had already represented England in five full internationals.

When his Stamford Bridge career ended 11 seasons later, he had added greatly to those achievements.

Undoubtedly, the arrival of Glenn Hoddle as Chelsea manager in 1993 was a focal point in Wise's career, fundamentally altering and extending his role

Up to that point he had operated mainly down the wings. Now he was the midfield general which revealed a vision enabling him to spray accurate passes over a wide range and unlocking gaps in opposition defences.

His reading of the game took him easily into open spaces and created his own goalscoring opportunities, as well as being a provider of his colleagues.

He took corners with deadly accuracy in front of wild cheers from his fan club at Stamford Bridge, and with less complimentary music when on enemy territory.

His honours list at Chelsea is formidable: FA Cup winners' medals in 1997 and 2000; European Cup-winners' and UEFA Super Cup trophies in 1998; the now almost discredited Football League Cup, together with the FA Charity Shield also in 2000. A truly golden age in CFC history.

Twenty-one caps for England was a surprisingly modest haul for one of his influence and ability. But in their wisdom the managers of the national side chose not to exploit his real strength, almost always using him as a winger and very rarely allowing him to be the midfield commander where his talents were crying out to be displayed.

Then, too, they were wary of his volatile temperament, and lack of self-discipline under pressure. At such moments it is a pity he could not have aped Hughie Gallacher and voluntarily removed himself to the touchline for a moment or two's cooling off.

The fittest player at the club, he captained Chelsea on more occasions than any other player in history and was enormously respected simply for what he was, and not least by his world famous colleagues flooding English football from Europe and beyond.

Returning to Stamford Bridge after five months away, to play against Chelsea for his new club, Leicester City, in October 2001, for maybe his final bow, he again stole the show.

Emerging from the tunnel minutes before kick-off, he was acclaimed by a choir of 40,000 voices who silenced the chairman ready at his microphone to present a silver box as a memento.

The game itself was largely forgettable, with Chelsea cruising to a 2-0 win. Every contribution from Wise was rapturously acknowledged before the curtain came down and, once more Dennis paraded before his adoring audience, reluctant to leave the stage where he had spent so many triumphant and happy times.

Wise left Leicester controversially and later signed for Millwall.

Chelsea Career

434-11 appearances   76 goals

Vic Woodley – better than Bonetti?

THE arguments still continue: Chelsea's greatest goalkeeper – Woodley or Bonetti? Vic or Peter? Suffice to say that each was of the very highest calibre in his own day.

Today, probably more so than ever before, managers require a strong squad of players with every position covered in case of emergency, thanks to the increased speed of the game escalating injuries.

Throughout the 1930s Chelsea had their goalkeeping options in the safe hands of Vic Woodley of England (19 caps) and Johnny Jackson of Scotland (eight caps).

Looking back, it is surprising that when out of favour, each was apparently content with Combination football. Also strange was the fact that neither attracted interest from other clubs.

In fact, Woodley was the declared the overwhelming winner with 272 games to his rival's 51.

Keeping goal for Chelsea in the 1930s was a particularly demanding occupation. The club seemed intent on bringing international forwards to Stamford Bridge at every possible opportunity, while the defence was left to get by as best it could.

It is no exaggeration to say that, but for Woodley's outstanding goalkeeping during that period, Chelsea would never have steered clear of relegation.

He was 19 when he stepped into the senior side as a young, untried professional. Previously he had learned his trade with Windsor & Eton, following a spell in Wiltshire village football.

He was simply the complete goalkeeper. He studied his job from every possible angle; he never stopped thinking about his craft. On cold days he rubbed his hands with oil of wintergreen; he was one of the first to adopt rubber studs and he was meticulous in his choice of gloves.

He was wonderfully sure in plucking high crosses from the air, an expert in narrowing the angle for breakaway forwards, and he exuded a confidence that spread throughout his defence

Vic Woodley also was supreme in international football and playing for England in 19 consecutive internationals (a spell ended only by the outbreak of World War Two), he kept at bay challenges from such as Harry Hibbs and Frank Swift.

When World War Two began, Woodley was engaged on vital war work rather than being conscripted into the services. The England selectors, however, confined their choices to HM Forces and Woodley never again represented his country.

Available for most of the ensuing seven seasons, he shared the duties of guarding the net at Stamford Bridge with Jackson before the manager, with an eye to the future, cast his eye elsewhere.

Almost Woodley's last Chelsea game, and in some ways the most famous of all, was against Moscow Dynamo in November 1945 when a crowd estimated at 100,000 invaded Stamford Bridge.

The following month he was put out to grass, seemingly to wind down his career in the West Country, with Bath City.

But not quite. There was to be a fairytale ending. After three months came an SOS from Derby County, who were experiencing an injury crisis in their goalkeeping department. Vic Woodley, of course not cup-tied, moved back into the limelight and gained a winner's medal against Charlton at Wembley before continuing to make some 30 League appearances for the Rams in 1946–47.

It was a wonderful final curtain for one of the finest of all England's goalkeepers.

Chelsea Career

272 appearances

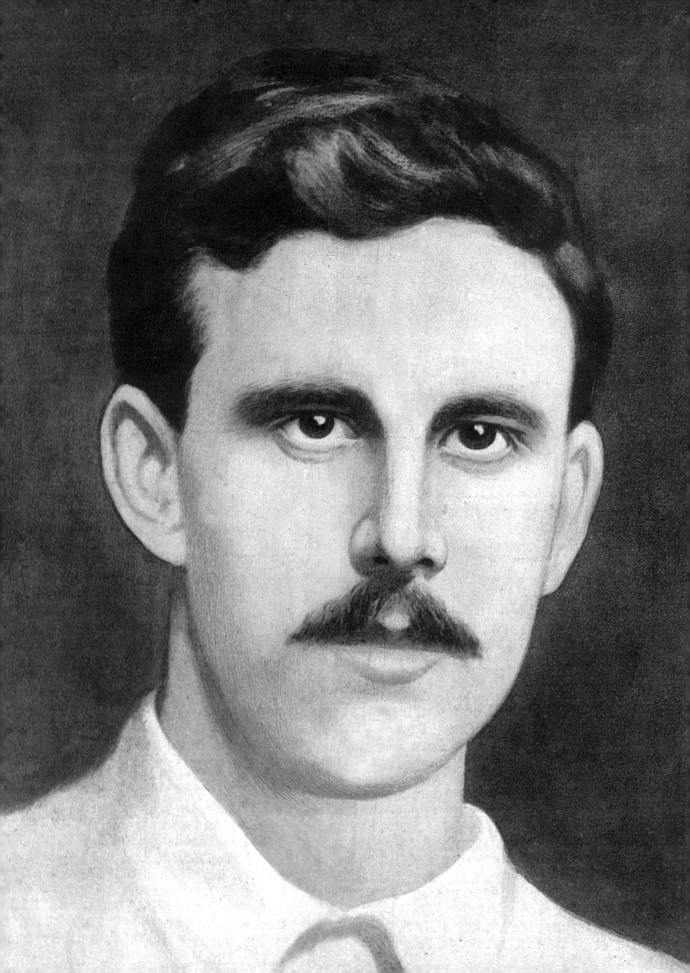

Vivian Woodward – the player with the magic boots

FROM 'Jock' Kirwan, who figured at outside-left in Chelsea's first-ever season, and indeed in the club's first-ever fixture, to Gus Poyet, there have been close connections and a frequent interchange of players between Stamford Bridge and Tottenham's White Hart Lane.

For many of the early years, the most frequently mentioned name in this respect was Vivian John Woodward, simply referred to by his contemporaries – and even later generations – as 'the greatest of them all'.

There is no purpose to advance this claim and to compare 'VJ' with present-day forwards. Suffice to say he was pre-eminent in his own day.

Twenty-three times did he play for England in full internationals – and 38 times for England Amateurs. On 16 occasions he was his country's choice in the Home International Tournament, in which, of course the participants, were mainly professionals.

Yet he was a true amateur in every sense of the word.

'A human chain of lighting; the footballer with magic in his boots.' There were just some of the epithets.

Playing, as he did so frequently, in the professional game, he never lost his own individual style more associated with unpaid performers.

He would pick up a loose ball and take it on half the length of the field on his own bypassing opponents en route.

But such excursions were by way of variety. He could swing the ball out to the wings and be on hand to score with a header as well as any of his professional teammates.

As his reputation grew he became an increasingly marked man and less time he was given to work himself into a scoring position. As a result a large percentage of his goals came from headers.

For as he once said, "It is much easier to evade a policeman when the ball is in the air, especially when you have the advantage of an inch or two in height."

Woodward's career began with his home club, Chelmsford, before he spent five seasons at Tottenham Hotspur (18 goals from 33 games) starting in 1908–09. Then he made his Chelsea debut in November 1909, playing whenever available, until World War One closed down normal football.

He had began mainly as a centre-forward, but soon found that his somewhat frail physique could not stand up to the physical buffetings in the professional game. Also, space was more easily acquired in the inside-forward positions and it was playing in that role that he picked up the majority of his international honours. Seldom was he absent through injury, claiming that a sense of balance enabled him to avoid hard knocks from heavier opponents. And he claimed also that he preferred playing in the Football League to amateur football with the Corinthians.

During his six seasons at Chelsea he was an automatic choice for the first team, yet other calls on his services allowed him to appear in less than half the fixtures in three seasons.

After the outbreak of World War One, he was one of the first to enlist in the Army. This limited his availability to a mere half a dozen occasions in a season when Chelsea were grinding their way to their first FA Cup Final .

His replacement was Jimmy Croal, a Scotsman from Glasgow who, along with Bob Thomson, filled the gap. Then, within days of the Final, Woodward was granted special leave from his Army duties, to the obvious delight of Chelsea officials, supporters and teammates alike.

There was a doubt about the fitness of Thomson almost right up to kick-off, before he was ultimately declared sound enough to play. Despite all the pressure which was brought to bear on him, Woodward would not budge. "If Bob Thomson is fit, I'm not playing, He has helped to put Chelsea into the Final – and deserves to play in the Final."

Woodward donned the blue shirt on only two more occasions in unofficial wartime regional football, after the Armistice had been signed. He was then nearing the age of 40. He served the club as a director from 1922 until 1930, but his memory as a player lived on. When Leslie Knighton was appointed manager in 1933, conscious of Chelsea's past he remembered the club's 'greatest attacker – a quicksilver leader...'

This great gentleman footballer of the early years of the century, died in February 1954 at the age of 74.

Chelsea Career

116 appearances   34 goals

Gianfranco Zola – Chelsea's greatest ever?

FROM the day Gianfranco Zola made his Chelsea debut in November 1996, at Blackburn, it was clear that one of the club's all-time greats had stepped on to the stage.

Zola's football pedigree was impeccable. Born in Sardinia, his apprenticeship had begun with Napoli, under the eye of Diego Maradona.

Next stop was Parma, where having endured the disappointments of losing to Arsenal in the European Cup-winners' Cup Final, 12 months later he was in the side which won a UEFA Cup winners' medal.

In the English Premiership his impact was immediate, and if during the latter management of Gianluca Vialli it seemed as if he was not destined to prolong his stay, ultimately it was the manager who moved away.

By then, not only was Zola a vital part of the Chelsea team – and idolised by the fans – he was integrated into the life of the capital along with his wife and children.

He had already won 33 caps for Italy before arriving in England although aged 31, his skills showed no signs of waning.

His mastery of the ball was complete. Played to him from any direction, at any angle, it was instantly under his control, his feet appearing to act as a magnet.

Even in the most confined spaces he was rarely dispossessed, weaving his way past defenders with extraordinary sleight of foot.

His territory embraced virtually the entire pitch, inch-perfect passes unlocking the most well-organised defences. And, of course, he was a regular goalscorer.

Some came from free-kicks, anything from up to 35 yards frequently defeating the most carefully marshalled defenders. Others were from superb solo efforts, some of which are permanently implanted into the memory.

His back-heel flick from a confined space, and hemmed in by opponents buzzing round him, in an FA Cup-tie against Norwich City at Stamford Bridge resulting in a goal, astounded his own colleagues as well as the opposition. Another after he had initiated an attack with a 40-yard pass against Manchester United was completed, three moves later, when he arrived on the scene to slip the ball into the net past a bemused goalkeeper.

In fact, the catalogue of such efforts is endless and every Chelsea fan will treasure his own particular favourites.

In the spring of 2002, his future with the club was in doubt. Approaching the age of 36, he had found himself too frequently for his own liking relegated to the substitutes bench.

He realised he was at a crossroads and family considerations also entered into the equation. But, undertaking an arduous, self-imposed summer training programme in Sardinia, he returned possibly fitter and even more determined than ever before.

His reunion with the manager, Claudio Ranieri, was another relevant factor. Soon his decision was amply justified, leading Chelsea's list of goalscorers and being voted Player of the Month for October 2002.

Not normally given to extravagant statement, Ranieri added his own feelings. "This has been one of his best seasons at Chelsea... he is fantastic." In July 2003 Chelsea fans were sad to see Zola leave Stamford Bridge for Cagliari.

Along with Dennis Wise, no Chelsea player has found his way into the hearts of the club's fans more readily since Jimmy Greaves.

Chelsea Career

260-51 appearances   80 goals